TEARS FOR THE NATION
STUDIES IN JEREMIAH & LAMENTATIONS

by Hal Hammons

OneStone
BIBLICAL RESOURCES

Published by:
One Stone Press
979 Lovers Lane
Bowling Green, KY 42103

Printed in the United States of America

ISBN (10 Digit): 1-941422-23-3
ISBN (13 Digit): 978-1-941422-23-6

Supplemental Materials Available:
PowerPoint slides for each lesson
Downloadable PDF

ONE STONE

BIBLICAL RESOURCES

1.800.428.0121

www.onestone.com

Table of Contents

For Mike,
who heard me say Ezekiel was my favorite prophet,
and then let me marry his daughter anyway.

Lesson 1
The Message
Jeremiah 1

God had a message for His people. It was not a pleasant one. It was not a strikingly original one. It was the same message of destruction and condemnation that had been delivered by prophet after prophet throughout the history of God's people, dating all the way back to Moses. And just as the people had ignored Moses, and Samuel, and Elijah, and Joel, and Isaiah, now they would ignore Jeremiah. But if the people of that day did not choose to save themselves, we can. Even though the Babylonians are not threatening to uproot our nation today, sin is as big a threat as it ever has been. Perhaps it is too much to ask for us to save our nation – but at least we can be warned in time to save ourselves.

The Origin of "Judah" as a Nation

To understand Jeremiah and the destruction of Judah properly, we have to appreciate the destruction of its sister nation, the northern tribes collectively known as Israel. To understand how "Israel" came to refer to a nation other than the one centered in Jerusalem, adhering to the lineage of David and maintaining the temple of Solomon, we need to go back in time a bit.

Saul was the first king of Israel. After 40 years and a brief power struggle for succession, David, the man who God Himself through Samuel would call "a man after His own heart" (1 Samuel 13:14), took the throne. God promised He would establish David's throne forever (2 Samuel 7:12-13) – a promise fulfilled eventually in the spiritual kingdom of Jesus, but at the time giving David assurance that his family would remain on the throne perpetually. God had every intention of keeping up His end of the covenant. But David's son, Solomon, rejected Him for the idols brought to him by his foreign wives. As a result, the prophet Ahijah spoke to Solomon's servant Jeroboam and promised him that he would reign over the majority of the 12 tribes of Israel (1 Kings 11:26-37). Then when Rehoboam, Solomon's son, proved unwise, only the tribes of Judah and Benjamin remained faithful, the others defecting to create a new nation under Jeroboam. For this reason, in Jeremiah and many other sections of the Old Testament, "Israel" refers to the northern division of the nation and "Judah" to the southern. That is the way the names will be used in this book.

What was the real cause of division in Israel? _____
_____
_____

Assyria, Babylon, or Neither?

Jeroboam had been promised a perpetual kingdom much as David had been. But he imme-diately erected golden calves in Bethel and Dan, proclaiming them the gods that delivered the nation from Egypt (1 Kings 12:28-29). God removed His protection from Jereboam's house, and the son who followed him on the throne was assassinated by Baasha, who reigned in his place. Multiple kings from multiple families followed, none of whom com-mitted themselves to the one true God. In the end, in the days of Hoshea (around 722-721

B.C.), the Assyrian king came and captured Samaria. He scattered the people throughout his empire, causing the northern tribes to be lost forever (2 Kings 17:6).

Assyria did not stop at Judah's border. Soon after the fall of Samaria, Sennacherib led his forces into the southern kingdom, ransacking city after city, finally laying siege to Jerusalem itself. Hezekiah, who had refused to continue paying tribute to Assyria as his father had done, laid out the threats of the Assyrians before the Lord and prayed for deliverance; God heard him, and the angel of God struck dead 185,000 Assyrian troops in a single night, leaving Sennacherib to take what was left of his army back home (Isaiah 37).

Soon afterward, Hezekiah was struck with a fatal illness. The prophet Isaiah told him to set his house in order. Again Hezekiah was moved to prayer; again God listened, promising him 15 more years of life. Unfortunately, he used those years to make an alliance with the Babylonians. Isaiah told him this choice would determine the future of the nation. If Hezekiah put his confidence in Babylon, it would be Babylon's hands in which the nation would rest (Isaiah 38-39). From this point forward, political forces in Judah can be lumped into two groups: the Jehovah party or Babylonian party, which respected the prophecy that tied the nation to Babylon; and the Egyptian/Assyrian party, which was constantly looking for ways to avoid the punishment promised by God.

Hezekiah's son, Manasseh, rejected God and turned to idols for most of his 55 years on the throne. His son Amon was so wicked that he was killed by his own servants – one of only two political assassinations in the history of Judah. As was the case after the death of Joash, the king's death was not used as an opportunity to put a usurper on the throne. Instead the rightful king (8-year-old Josiah, in the case of Amon's death) was placed on the throne. Josiah led the nation in numerous spiritual efforts, restoring the temple and finding the lost book of the law. Ultimately he died at the Battle of Megiddo trying to prevent Pharaoh Neco from supporting the Assyrians against Babylon (2 Kings 22-23).

Why do you think political assassinations were so rare in Judah and so common in Israel?

_____

_____

_____

The Sons of Josiah

The people chose the younger son, Jehoahaz, to be Josiah's successor in 612 B.C. Three months later Neco returned to Jerusalem, took Jehoahaz with him to Egypt, and put his older brother Jehoiakim on the throne – who presumably would run the kingdom more to Egypt's liking. Three years later, though, Nebuchadnezzar led Babylonian troops into Jerusalem and forced Jehoiakim into subjugation. Along with tribute, Nebuchadnezzar took the cream of Judah's royal families back with him to serve in his court – including Daniel, Shadrach, Meshach and Abed-nego (Daniel 1:1-8). This marked the beginning of 70 years of Babylonian captivity, as Jeremiah would prophesy (Jeremiah 24:12).

Why did God allow Josiah to die? Would Judah's fortunes not have been much better if he had survived? _____

_____

_____

When Jehoiakim died, his son Jehoiachin assumed the throne. (He is the one called Coniah in Jeremiah 22:24-30 and Jeconiah in Matthew 1:12). But just three months later Nebuchadnezzar returned to Jerusalem. He took Jehoiachin back to Babylon in chains and installed his uncle, Zedekiah, on the throne in his place. With Jehoiachin he also took 10,000 other captives; this is the second stage of Babylonian captivity (2 Kings 24:10-16, Ezekiel 1:1-3).

Why were these kings punished for rebelling against pagan oppressors when Hezekiah was praised for it? _____
_____
_____

Finally, after 11 years of support from Babylon, Zedekiah also rebelled. Nebuchadnezzar came for the third time in 587 B.C. and completely razed Jerusalem, leveling the temple and taking most of the people captive. This is the third stage of captivity. He appointed Gedaliah to govern in the absence of a royal family; however, Gedaliah was assassinated by rebels led by Ishmael, son of Nethaniah. The rebels fled to Egypt to escape the wrath of Babylon, against Jeremiah's warnings, taking with them whoever Nebuchadnezzar had left behind (including Jeremiah himself). But even in Egypt, Jeremiah continued to prophesy against the ones who had rejected God and pronounced doom against all nations that had rebelled against His rule – including Egypt.

Why were the people so confident they could succeed against Babylon? _____
_____
_____

Introducing Jeremiah

Judging from the length of time he prophesied and from his reference to himself as a "youth," Jeremiah must have been relatively young when called into service as a prophet. The first few verses of the prophecy introduce him simply as "the son of Hilkiah, of the priests who were in Anathoth in the land of Benjamin." Anathoth was one of the towns in Benjamin given to the priests in Joshua 21:18. Benjamin being small and traditionally allied with Judah, it remained loyal to Rehoboam and the family of David when the split occurred.

He was called in the 13th year of Josiah, but few references are made in his prophecy to work done during Josiah's reign. The bulk of his work was done in front of kings that were not nearly as receptive to his work as Josiah would have been. Judging from the prominence Jeremiah held and the difficulty the kings had in ridding themselves of him, it is reasonable to assume Jeremiah became ensconced in the Jerusalem political scene in the last 18 years of Josiah's reign, much as Isaiah had done a century before. He would be the chief spokesman in favor of peaceably accepting judgment from God at the hands of the Babylonians. The opposition, though, ever proud, generally preferred to provide a course to safety for themselves that did not depend on repentance and submission. As a result, Jeremiah was constantly bounced back and forth between factions, occasionally respected and honored but never really trusted or heeded.

Why would God bother sending a prophet to such a rebellious nation? _____
_____
_____
_____

Jeremiah's Story:
Called from the Womb

God needed a messenger. He found one in a young priest from Anathoth. But He was looking long before Jeremiah knew. In fact, the first words God spoke to the young prophet appear to be these:

"Before I formed you in the womb I knew you, and before you were born I consecrated you" (Jeremiah 1:5). Besides addressing the topic of individuality, identity and personhood prior to birth (always a relevant discussion in our abortion-crazed society), this tells us that God had a particular plan in mind for Jeremiah before he was even born. The ability of God to put wheels in motion well in advance to accomplish His plan should not surprise Bible students. Abraham's family was being prepared four centuries in advance to punish the native tribes of Canaan (Genesis 15:16-21). Cyrus the Great was called by name a hundred years before his birth as the one "anointed" for greatness that would be worked on behalf of God's people (Isaiah 44:28-45:7).

What other Bible characters were born to a particular destiny? Does this rob them of their free will? _____
_____
_____

Yes, Jeremiah was young. But that would not make a difference in God's plan. After all, the power is always in God, not the messenger. God promised, "I am with you to deliver you" (1:8). If Jeremiah limited himself to the words given to him by God, his age would be irrelevant with regard to the authority he would carry.

What other Bible characters received similar assurances? _____
_____
_____

Of course, carrying God's word would not, in and of itself, assure Jeremiah of a receptive audience. Quite the opposite, in fact. God promised him that the people would oppose him and his work strongly. Still, strength comes from God. Jeremiah would be "a fortified city ... a pillar of iron ... walls of bronze" against them. Whatever attack they might mount against him, the protection provided by God would be more than sufficient.

What other prophet from this time was hardened this way? _____
_____
_____

Key Image: The Almond Rod (1:11-12)

Occasionally a knowledge of the original language of the text can provide an insight unavailable any other way. Such is the case with the word almond. The Hebrew word, shaqed, is almost identical to the word for watching, shoqed. The play on words, invisible in English, is obvious in Hebrew; as Jeremiah sees the almond rod, so God is watching His people. It may also bring our thoughts to Numbers 17, where Aaron's priesthood was defended by God Himself. Each tribe of Israel chose a rod to represent itself and wrote on each a family name from that tribe – Aaron's name in the case of the rod for Levi. The next day, buds, blossoms, and eventually ripe almonds appeared on Aaron's rod. In both cases, God is shown to know fully who is approved and who is not, who is worthy of standing in His presence and who is not.

Key Image: The Boiling Pot (1:13-16)

If you have only the knowledge of Biblical geography that is provided by the maps in the back of your Bible, the constant admonitions for Israel to look for trouble coming from the north might be puzzling. After all, Assyria and Babylon would be more accurately described as being east of Palestine. But ride a camel or walk through this country and the image makes sense. The desert directly east of Israel would be almost impassable. The common route from Mesopotamia was to follow the Euphrates River north and west, and then ford the river near Carchemish. Therefore, invading tribes not coming from Egypt would almost certainly threaten from the north, just as God had indicated. God would indeed kindle a fire beneath the feet of Judah, and it would indeed come from the north.

Key Verse: Jeremiah 1:19

"They will fight against you, but they will not overcome you, for I am with you to deliver you," declares the LORD.

Key Lessons

* *Accept the job God gives you.* Obedience is your responsibility, not success.
* *God's word is sovereign over any earthly power.* With God's word in our mouths, we can exercise authority over anyone and anything in His name.
* *Opposition is certain.* God will give us the victory in His time and His way

Lesson 2
Faithfulness
Jeremiah 2 - 5

Repeatedly in the Bible, Old and New Testaments alike, God's relationship with His people is compared to a marriage. Regrettably, many marriages end in divorce. And God's marriage to Judah, like many marriages, reached that point because of unfaithfulness – more specifically, Judah's constant involvement with other gods. God had promised to be faithful to Judah, and He had; beginning with the deliverance from Egypt, continuing through the times of judges and the kingdom of David, and all the way up to Hezekiah and deliverance from the Assyrians. God had sheltered His people from harm. But this only was the case when they agreed to be sheltered. Judah's rebellion had gotten so constant and unapologetic, God was going to chasten His beloved in a way she had never experienced before. It would not be pleasant, but hopefully Judah would return and the marriage could be saved.

The Wayward Wife

Betrothals, or what we would call engagements, worked somewhat differently in Bible times. For legal purposes, committing yourself to marriage made you married. As with Joseph and Mary (Luke 2:4-5), engaged couples would not have the privilege of the marriage bed but would have traveled together and been taxed together. The fulfilment of their contract was yet to come.

Likewise, our commitment to God permits us to wear the name of Christ before the marriage is consummated. Jesus plans to present to Himself "the church in all her glory" (Ephesians 5:27) after judgment, but we are not ready yet; we need to make wedding day preparations with regard to holiness, purity and noble conduct.

How tragic it was, then, that Judah, the espoused one of God, had rejected the love of her youth. She was willing to follow God through the wilderness to escape Egypt, all the way to the Promised Land. But after arriving, the people "walked after emptiness and became empty" (2:5). By Jeremiah's day the state of the nation had worsened to the point that the bride-to-be had entirely forgotten her true love – as silly a condition as an actual bride forgetting the details of her wedding day (2:32). She considered herself "free to roam" (2:31). In fact, she is told, "even the wicked women you have taught your ways" (2:33). The prostitutes had something to learn, it would seem, from the fornicating ways of the people of God.

What does it mean to be betrothed to God? _____

_____

_____

What Nation Rejects Its Gods?

The pagans at least had this going for them: they were loyal. The Philistines could be counted on to serve Dagon. The Syrians had Baal and Ashtoreth. The Egyptians had their pantheon of deities. And generally speaking, they were faithful to them. It is ironic, then, that the nation that worshiped the one true God would be the one that would be unfaithful (2:9-11). God compares Judah's rebellion to those who would quit drinking from the fresh water of an Artesian well, straight from the aquifer, for a muddy cistern that could not even properly hold the water someone placed in it (2:13). Even at the time of Jeremiah's criticism of their infidelity, the nation's leaders were busy trying to make alliances against the will of God with foreign nations such as Egypt and Assyria – to drink their waters (2:18). And of course, alliances such as these traditionally were accompanied by idolatrous ceremonies.

Yes, in a sense, God had made them free – but free to serve Him, not free to do as they pleased. Israel was like a female slave in Egypt, kept in chains. God freed Israel through Moses, giving the Israelites privileges and blessings they had never known in this new marriage relationship. But God did not release them from slavery just so they could be freed; He bought Israel so she could be devoted to Him and Him alone. You would think that her gratitude would be such that she would eagerly embrace this new, loving relationship. But no. "I will not serve," she arrogantly said (2:20), and eagerly gave herself to any suitor who happened along.

Jeremiah described Judah as a wild donkey that had the opportunity to wear shoes and be taken care of by a loving owner. But the blessings God offered did not move her: "It is hopeless! No! For I have loved strangers, and after them I will walk" (2:25).

What "other gods" can we choose today? _____

_____

_____

God's Response

Considering that God's spiritual bride has already abandoned Him for another (actually, several others), what was He to do? Go on pretending nothing is wrong? Treat Judah like His spiritual bride when she was inventing new ways to break her covenant with Him? That would be as ridiculous as a husband trying to still be married to a woman he has already divorced (3:1). Instead He was going to increase His criticisms of her behavior and introduce new hardships, including drought, although such measures had not helped Judah find her shame (3:3).

In the early days of Jeremiah's work, while Josiah still lived, God was already comparing Judah to her sister, Israel, which had been dispersed to the four winds of the earth by Assyria. It was common knowledge that God had done this as a response to her harlotries; God thought that perhaps his constant chastening of her sister to the north would encourage Judah to become faithful again; instead she followed faithfully in her sister's footsteps (3:6-10). Because of this, God told Jeremiah, "Faithless Israel has proved herself more righteous than treacherous Judah" (3:11).

Therefore, God issued a call for faithless Israel to return – no doubt to remind Judah that she, too, could be reconciled to Him. He was still eager to welcome His people home as long as she would repent and obey (3:12-13). He spoke of a day in which Judah and Israel could be united again under spiritual shepherds, living in fellowship with one another and with Him (3:15-18). This can be seen as a potential reunion based on true repentance that has never been realized; however, a spiritual fulfillment is possible as well. In the gospel era, all people everywhere, regardless of their background or the depth of their depravity, are welcome to come to "Zion" (Isaiah 2:1-4) and receive every blessing in the heavenly places (Ephesians 1:3).

How does God heal faithlessness (3:22)? Is it all His doing, or do we have a role? _____

_____

_____

A Wind Too Strong

Wind isn't necessarily a bad thing. Wheat threshers of the day would toss grain into the air and allow the breeze to carry dust away and leave only the grain. Even strong winds can serve a purpose by breaking off dead leaves and branches, allowing for new growth to emerge. But the "scorching wind" coming to Jerusalem was not that sort of wind (4:11-12). This wind would represent the wrath of God – a tornado, wreaking havoc and leaving nothing in its wake. "Disaster on disaster is proclaimed, for the whole land is devastated" (4:20). The destruction reaches the point of making the earth "formless and void" (4:23), which takes us back to the very beginning of creation in Genesis 1:1-2. It is as though God was taking Judah back to the very beginning with His wrath, hoping a clean slate might provide for a better outcome. After all, as Jeremiah says repeatedly, He would not "execute a complete destruction" (4:27). There would be a chance to rebuild.

While the winds rage with the wrath of God, He asks, "And you, O desolate one, what will you do?" (4:30). This rebellious wife can dress herself up, paint her face gaudy, and make overtures to as many suitors as she can find. In the end, Judah would find how little these foreign nations really regarded her. In fact, the alliances Judah had made with foreign powers would be precisely the tools God would use to bring down Judah.

Why is God's punishment compared to childbirth (4:31)? _____

_____

_____

Jeremiah's Story:
The "Utterly Deceived" People

God's message of condemnation and repentance has always been constant; it was still the same in Jeremiah's day – "'If you will return, O Israel,' declares the LORD, 'Then you should return to Me. And if you will put away your detested things from My presence, and will not waver, and you will swear, "As the LORD lives," in truth, in justice and in righteousness; then the nations will bless themselves in Him, and in Him they will glory'" (4:1-3).

What does it mean to circumcise the heart (4:4)? _____

_____

_____

While life remains, there is always opportunity to repent and reform. That is why Jeremiah and other prophets in similar circumstances exhorted their listeners to quit sin and return to God. But apart from any repentance on the people's part, God promised to bring "a destroyer of nations" (4:7) – a great enemy, determined to bring the nation to its knees. In that day, the hearts of the king and princes would fail, and the priests and prophets would be stunned into submission (4:9). On that day, it would be too late to turn back the consequences of rebellion simply by repenting.

What is the symbolism of sackcloth? _____
_____
_____

This was not the message the people had been getting prior to Jeremiah's call. Dismayed, Jeremiah exclaims to God, "Surely You have utterly deceived this people and Jerusalem, saying, 'You will have peace'; whereas a sword touches the throat" (4:10). But God does not and cannot lie (Titus 1:2). The message he was receiving directly from God by inspiration would override any impression he might have received from history or from the words of others. The threat was real; the sooner Jeremiah accepted it, the sooner he could begin warning others.

When had God promised peace to the people? Who was promising peace in Jeremiah's day? _____
_____
_____

Key Image: The First of His Harvest (2:3)

God made a spiritual investment in Judah, and through the centuries He had nurtured her growth much like a farmer would watch over his growing crops. "All who ate of it became guilty" (2:3). Judah – and before the split, the entire nation of Israel – was a people holy to God (Exodus 19:5-6, Deuteronomy 7:6). It was inappropriate for another nation to make spoil of her. The description of Judah being "the first of His harvest" reckons back to Leviticus 23:9-14, in which the first fruits of the harvest were devoted to God and were to be offered to Him instead of consumed. Tragically, though, the nation was not holy any longer. Apart from their devotion to God, the people had no reason to expect His protection.

Key Image: The Fountain of Living Waters (2:13)

Fresh, clean water is the foundation of life. Dating back to Moses in the wilderness, God had always provided water for His people – and, more importantly, spiritual refreshment for any who would have faith enough to drink it. Whenever the people trusted in God completely, He was faithful to supply their every need. It seems impossible that someone would drink out of a muddy hole in the ground instead of from a fresh spring, but that is what Judah had done by forsaking God for idols. Similar terminology is found in the New Testament for us as Christians; Jesus promises to create "a well of water springing up to eternal life" for those who come to Him for refreshment (John 4:13-14).

Key Verse: Jeremiah 5:31

The prophets prophesy falsely, and the priests rule on their own authority; and My people love it so! But what will you do at the end of it?

Key Lessons

- *Being "the people of God" is not enough*: We must continually strive to be worthy of His name
- *Sin is something to be ashamed of*. We can get so steeped in sin, we forget how humiliating it is.
- *Pleasant words are not a substitute for truth*: There is only "peace" when God says there is peace.

Lesson 3
Brokenness
Jeremiah 6 -10

The New King James version uses "hurt." The English Standard Version prefers "wounds." I am not enough of a scholar to weigh in as to which is more true to the original Hebrew. But for the context in Jeremiah, I prefer the New American Standard's word – "brokenness." The injuries of Judah were not merely superficial; the nation had become completely dysfunctional in its mission of honoring the God who had blessed and protected them faithfully for so long. Radical therapy would be necessary to effect a healing, and no good could come of Judah until that therapy was enacted and completed. Brokenness doesn't heal quickly, easily or painlessly.

The Wrath of God

It was not God who broke Judah. Judah broke herself. She was so far gone, she did not want to hear Jeremiah's words of warning. "Behold, the word of the LORD has become a reproach for them; they have no delight in it" (6:10). If the people were unwilling to listen to God's words of instruction, there was no way they could find their way back to Him.

Preaching to such ones was difficult for Jeremiah. God had promised it would be. But it was even more difficult to remain quiet. God's wrath became Jeremiah's wrath, and he felt compelled to pour it out on whoever might listen (6:11). It wasn't just a matter of whether it would do any good; Jeremiah could not live with himself and act otherwise.

The sin of the people was profound. God, through Jeremiah, detailed several specific examples in Jeremiah 6:13-15. First, "everyone is greedy for gain." Religious officials were giving the "prophecies" that would pay the best, and in so doing (at least in some instances) were intentionally subverting the truth. And this attitude was contagious; it had infected the nation "from the least of them even to the greatest of them."

Secondly, the problems the people were suffering – and, by extension, the sin that had brought them on – had been minimized. "Peace, peace," was the message, but that was not God's message. A message of imminent improvement is surely easier to swallow, but that sort of "solution" could not possibly heal the brokenness that was plaguing the nation.

Thirdly, the moral climate in the nation had reached disastrous levels. "They were not even ashamed at all; they did not even know how to blush." It takes a truly hardened sinner to not be embarrassed by sin; Judah had gone to even greater depths, though, not even realizing there was anything about which to be embarrassed. They had entirely forgotten what it meant to be holy.

How does a nation get to this depth of depravity? _____

_____

_____

The Vanity of Offerings

Let it not be said that Judah had abandoned the God of heaven entirely. Sacrifices continued in the temple; in fact, the people seemed to have been rather proud of the fact. Above all else, they still considered themselves God's chosen people. Apparently they did not see the disconnect between that and their idolatry. It would seem they thought God should be happy with them as long as they continued to make their appropriate sacrifices. God told Jeremiah to inform the people how wrong they were.

Leviticus describes many offerings. Most were eaten as part of the worship being offered. Some, "burnt offerings," were entirely consumed by the fire of the altar—as though God Himself was eating them. But God sarcastically suggests they should go ahead and eat it all (7:21). It is not as though the offerings satisfied God in any way; this was for the benefit of the people, to remind them of how much they owed to God. The call to holiness in worship is an echo of Isaiah's words a century before (Isaiah 1:11-15). Merely offering the sacrifices for the sake of having offered them misses the point.

Understanding the "not/but" phrase in Jeremiah 7:22-23 helps with the apparent contradiction regarding whether God commanded burnt offerings. A "not/but" phrase de-emphasizes the first element for the purpose of re-emphasizing the second. The most familiar example may be in John 6:27 – "Do not work for the food which perishes, but for the food which endures to eternal life." Jesus is not condemning physical work for physical food; He is simply saying it is not nearly as important as spiritual sustenance. Likewise, God is not denying the clear teaching of Exodus 29:10-25; burnt offerings were commanded at Sinai. But the priority was always obedience. That is why "Thou shalt never miss a sacrifice" was not one of the Ten Commandments. That is why Samuel told Saul "Behold, to obey is better than sacrifice, and to heed than the fat of rams" (1 Samuel 15:22).

Can our worship become vain today in the same way? Explain. _____
_____
_____

The Delusion of Idols

It is difficult for us to relate to idol worship today. The plain sense of passages such as Jeremiah 10:1-10 is undeniable, and it boggles the mind that anyone would think otherwise. Yet Judah did, despite having a long heritage of reciting the deeds of the true God who needed no physical representation.

Jeremiah gets quite specific with the limitations of idols. They do not appear on their own; a craftsman must cut a tree down or dig a stone up, and then carve it appropriately. They are not attractive enough even then; they must be covered with silver and gold. These all-powerful gods must be carried to where the worshipers wish them to be, and then nailed into place so they will not fall over. This is worthy of worship?

It is no surprise that the prophecy of 10:11 has been fulfilled; the gods worshiped by the pagans have long since been assigned curiosity status. The God of heaven remains, however. The One who has consistently shown true power, who demonstrates His worth every day, is described in 10:12-14. It is quite a different picture than what was seen earlier. Humanity insults itself when it stoops to this level (10:14). And it certainly was beneath the dignity of the people of God to worship sticks and stones. "The portion of Jacob" (10:16) knew enough to acknowledge and revere the one true God – "The LORD of hosts is His name." Or at least, they should have known.

Why is the goldsmith put to shame by his idols? _____

_____

_____

The Destruction of Judah's Tent

In a culture such as Judah's, in which herding and nomadic travel were engrained into the national consciousness, one's "tent" was one's home. More than that, it was one's life. Everything of value except one's herds was in the tent. The tent kept the heat in and the predators out. But a tent is, in the end, just a tent. Even with the best of plans, materials and maintenance, it can be destroyed in an instant. That was what was happening to Judah as Jeremiah watched, powerless to do anything about it. It was, as he said, a sickness that he had to bear (10:19).

In times past, there may have been hope on the horizon. Perhaps insiders such as Isaiah may have endured an evildoer such as Amon because they saw spiritual worth in Hezekiah, who would come afterward. As hard as Amon might work to destroy the tent, Hezekiah could be trusted to at least attempt to put it together again. Such was not the case in the wake of Josiah's death. Three sons followed Josiah to the throne, each just as bad as the one that went before. It is not surprising, then, that Jeremiah would say, almost speaking on Josiah's behalf, "My sons have gone out from me and are no more. There is no one to stretch out my tent again or to set up my curtains" (10:20).

Things were made even worse by the failure of the "shepherds" of the people – those responsible for their spiritual care. As true shepherds would be devoted to the welfare of the sheep, so too the priests and prophets were to make sure the people knew the ways of God and were motivated to walk in them. Unfortunately, Jeremiah wrote, "the shepherds have become stupid and have not sought the LORD; therefore they have not prospered, and all their flock is scattered" (11:21). With rotten leadership inside the tent and uncaring, ungodly leadership out among the sheep, Judah was on an irreversible slide downward. Soon, the so-called leadership would be put to the fire for testing when "a great commotion out of the land of the north" (10:22) would threaten everything. According to Jeremiah, there was not much doubt as to what the outcome would be.

What are "shepherds" in the church today, and what is their function? _____

_____

_____

Jeremiah's Story:
The Temple of the LORD

Often "Zion" or "Jerusalem" is used symbolically to represent the nation. Partly because Jerusalem was the city of David, the center of social and political activity in Israel. But mostly because the temple was in Jerusalem. The temple symbolized the presence of God. The presence of God set Israel (and, in the days of the divided kingdom, Judah) apart from every other nation. It was a daily reminder not only of who God was, but also of who they were.

So when Jeremiah stood at the gate of the temple and proclaimed the downfall of the nation, it was received as heresy. Defiling the holy structure with a message of abandonment and loss was profane. Without the temple, Judah would be just the same as any other nation – forsaken by God, unclean in His sight, without hope.

That, of course, was precisely the point.

"Do not trust in deceptive words, saying, 'This is the temple of the LORD, the temple of the LORD, the temple of the LORD,'" Jeremiah warned them (7:4). Safety is found in God's presence, not God's building. Buildings come and go. And if the people had forgotten that, they needed to remember Shiloh. Shiloh, of course, was the permanent resting place of the tabernacle, the forerunner of the temple that accompanied Israel through the wilderness. But Shiloh was destroyed, and the tabernacle (presumably) along with it. Psalm 78:60-64 also refers to the tragedy. It is assumed that this refers to the incident in 1 Samuel 4, in which the ark of the covenant was taken into battle and subsequently lost. If God could abandon Shiloh, and if He could abandon Ephraim (7:15), He could abandon Judah as well, temple and all.

Was "innocent blood" ever literally shed in the temple? Cite references. _____

_____

_____

That said, the whole purpose of Jeremiah's preaching implies that the tide could still be turned. If they would change, God said through Jeremiah, "I will let you dwell in this place" (7:3). Although likely already captive to Babylon in a sense (the chronology is often nonspecific in Jeremiah), Judah could be largely left in place. Large-scale deportations need not happen.

Would relenting mean God was breaking His promise to punish Judah? _____

_____

_____

But things would have to change. In lieu of true repentance, though, Jeremiah was not to make entreaties for them (7:16). God had no intention of saving people who were determined to be lost. Men, women and children alike were busy about the task of rebelling against Him – almost to spite Him. But no amount of insult could actually harm God; it was only themselves whom they were harming.

When does God quit hearing entreaties for the wicked? _____

_____

_____

Key Image: the Balm of Gilead (8:22)

Gilead, an area just east of the Jordan River, had been famous far and wide for the medicinal herbs and plants that grew there. Medicines were being formed from them and exported to Egypt as early as Joseph's time (Genesis 37:25). The assumption, of course, would be that the patient would get better after getting the medicine. But Jeremiah's "patient," Judah, continued to worsen in spiritual health month after month (8:20-21). The problem, of course, was not a lack of medicine, but rather (as is often the case with stubborn patients) an unwillingness to take it. He looked ahead to a time when the nation would call out from captivity, wondering how God could have abandoned His people so completely – and when God would respond with yet another condemnation of their idolatry (8:18-19). This prophecy would be fulfilled in short order when the nation would be carried away into Babylonian captivity

Key Image: Circumcised and yet Uncircumcised (9:25-26)

Throughout the Old and New Testaments, the act of circumcision as practiced in Israel is portrayed as a symbol of purification. Just as the literal operation removes the excess, so also the people were required to circumcise their hearts (Deuteronomy 10:16; Jeremiah 4:4). As the operation testified to the faith of Abraham which preceded his faith, so also we who share his faith share in his commitment to holiness (Romans 4:9-12).

But circumcision is not the same as holiness. Many nations, some of which had roots in Abraham themselves, practiced circumcision; however, they were not people of faith, and no one – least of all the people of Judah – expected God to treat them as people of faith. And just as God's judgment would ultimately fall on the pagans, so also He would judge His own people who had taken comfort in the flesh instead of in true submission and obedience.

Key Verse: Jeremiah 10:23

I know, O LORD, that a man's way is not in himself, nor is it in a man who walks to direct his steps.

Key Lessons

- *Real solutions for real problems.* Simply declaring oneself at peace with God is not enough.
- *God will refine His people.* Hardship shows us for what we truly are.
- *Greatness is not measured in shallow terms.* A well-dressed rock or stick is still a rock or a stick.

Lesson 4
Drought
Jeremiah 11 - 16

Nothing puts the average person more in the hand of God than rain. Without rain, there are no crops. Without crops, he starves. And there is absolutely nothing he can do to bring the rain. So when God chose to bring drought in the days of Jeremiah, as He did in the days of Elijah a century or so before (1 Kings 17:1; James 5:17), the people took notice. They had to. But they did not have to turn back to God after their chastening. They could choose to remain in their depravity. And that is exactly what they did.

The Cry of Jerusalem

It requires no faith to mourn in difficult circumstances. The mere fact that Jerusalem cried out in the midst of drought does not imply that they had been brought to repentance. But that was the purpose of God's rebuke. Jeremiah's words along with God's actions should have been enough for the people to repent and return to Him. Sadly, they were not.

The nobles, tasked with the welfare of the nation, sent their servants out to retrieve whatever water might be found (14:3). But the symbolism of 2:13 proved to be all too literal. Cisterns had been dug to catch rainwater and retain whatever groundwater might seep in. But the earth was deeply cracked from a lack of moisture (14:4). Not only had there been no rain, whatever water might have been in the ground already had dried up. The servants returned with their vessels empty. And although the shame and humiliation seen in 14:3 might literally have been attached to the servants themselves, surely it must have been shared with the nobles. They had failed. The problem was far deeper than rainfall, though. God had withheld the rain because Judah had withheld her heart.

Jeremiah, who was suffering along with the rest of Judah, pleaded with God to bring back the rain. He acknowledged Judah's guilt and begged for mercy, saying that God had become like a stranger to the land by pulling back (14:7-9). He asks, "Why are You like a man dismayed, like a mighty man who cannot save?" And God answers, with information Jeremiah already had. The people "loved to wander" (14:10), He said. And although Jeremiah's own penitence is surely not in question, he makes no mention of any national return to God. And God was not going to forgive a nation that had not repented. "Do not pray for the welfare of this people," God says (14:11). Further petitions would be wasted on them. Circumstances would worsen, not improve.

Where should the nobles have searched for water (v.3)? What should have been their true source of shame? _____
_____
_____

The "Flowing" Land

Talk of a "flowing" land must have sounded wonderful to Israel in the wilderness. A land that produced its own food, that provided ample foraging for livestock, that would not require supernatural assistance from God to support a nation – such would have been a blessed change for them. And this is what God promised them – "a land flowing with milk and honey, as it is this day" (11:5). Not only did He give them a bountiful land, that land was still just as bountiful as it ever had been. But no land is prosperous without rain. And the drought that God had brought upon the land had canceled out the blessing of the land itself. Judah's reversal of fortune was not because the land or God Himself had changed; it came from the nation's rejection of Him. He had kept his part of the covenant—and He would continue to do so if the nation would go back to keeping its part."

It had become convenient for Judah to forget, though, that the covenant needed to be kept on both ends. They had counted on God keeping His end of the bargain through all of their spiritual infidelities over the years, and in some measure He had. But His patience and forbearance was almost gone. Now God was looking to keep the rest of the bargain He had struck with Israel through Moses – "all the words of this covenant" (11:8), not just the words of hope and reward. The covenant had also spoken repeatedly of the consequences of rebellion. One such passage is Leviticus 26:14-39. God spoke in this text of waves of judgment exercised against a rebellious nation, including illness, plague, warfare and ultimately national disaster; "You, however, I will scatter among the nations and will draw out a sword after you, as your land becomes desolate and your cities become waste" (Leviticus 26:33). If the people would refuse to keep the Sabbath in the land, they would be taken out of the land.

In the final day of disaster, God said, there would be those who would at long last reach out to God for forgiveness and mercy. But it would be too late in that day (11:11). God's hand would not draw back. And, to show the hypocrisy of such "repentance," God said they would respond to His rejection with even further appeals to the foreign gods to whom they had become so attached. But such gods had no real power, and they certainly could not be relied upon to defeat the plans of a vengeful God.

When are physical blessings a sign of God's approval? _____

_____

_____

The Prosperity of the Wicked

As was the case with Jeremiah's contemporary, Habakkuk, Jeremiah was confused at the way God stayed His hand against evil. "Why has the way of the wicked prospered? Why are all those who deal in treachery at ease? You have planted them, they have also taken root; they grow, they have even produced fruit" (12:1-2). Although it is tempting to think Jeremiah is speaking of the prosperity of the Babylonians and other enemies of the nation, his reference to the land mourning "for the wickedness of those who dwell in it" (12:4) makes it clear that it is his fellow children of Abraham to whom he refers. God had been the One who had blessed them, just as He had blessed the righteous worthies of old. But He did so despite their "worship," not because of it – "You are near to their lips but far from their mind" (12:2). Whatever service they may have offered to Him was shallow and insincere.

Surely Jeremiah was expecting, or at least hoping for, words of comfort and explanation from his God in this time of spiritual turmoil. But God instead gave him the exact opposite sort of news. The challenge to faith Jeremiah faced was nothing compared to what would come in future days. "If you have run with footmen and they have tired you out, then how can you compete with horses? If you fall down in a land of peace, how will you do in the thicket of the Jordan" (12:5). Jeremiah was only getting started in his ministry; things would only get more difficult. God speaks of Jeremiah's own family turning against him, even though they may put on a façade of cordiality (12:6). The challenge to come, compared to what he faced then, would be like going from racing men to racing horses – like running through flat, peaceful terrain with difficulty to navigating "the thicket of the Jordan," full of lions and all manner of other hazards.

The solution was not to find meaning behind the current circumstances or the circumstances to come. As we see repeatedly in the Old Testament, the emphasis was on finding the strength through faith to deal with whatever adversity may come. If we do not toughen up to face the challenges of today, we will certainly be in no shape to face the disasters tomorrow may bring.

At what point have we suffered more than our fair share? At what point will God put a stop to it? _____

_____

_____

A Fresh Waistband

Often God required His prophets to live out His message in the flesh. Such was the case when He told Jeremiah to go to the Euphrates wearing a new, unwashed "linen waistband." (The Holman Christian Standard Bible, in an effort to help us understand a culture and style of dress very much unlike ours, uses the word "underwear.") Jeremiah was to buy a fresh, unwashed piece of linen, wrap it around himself, and travel to the Euphrates far away to the north. (Great effort has been made to identify the Euphrates as a river that is not hundreds of miles away; however, most conservative scholars seem willing to accept Jeremiah at his word.) Once he arrived, he was to put the fabric in a crevice and leave it there for "many days." Later, when he arrived to retrieve the waistband, the unstoppable forces of nature had wreaked havoc on it, rendering it completely unfit (13:1-7).

God makes the application for us in 13:8-11. At one point Judah had clung to God as closely as could be imagined. Their relationship was intimate. But separated from God and from the care He would take for His prize possession, Judah disintegrated into a useless mess, unfit for any service at all.

Judah's figurative trip to Assyria – overtures toward the fading power to the north in an effort to stave off God's judgment through the Babylonians – had destroyed any usefulness the nation might have had for its true God. At this point it made no more sense for God to hang onto Judah than it would for Jeremiah to pretend his waistband was still in pristine shape. Judah was no longer fit to be close to God, and so God would no longer be close to Judah.

Can we cling to God and idols at the same time? _____

_____

_____

A Life Without Family

Exactly how old Jeremiah was when he began his ministry is unclear, and the irregular timeline in the book makes determining his age at any given time even more difficult. But it would seem at least that Jeremiah was relatively young when he was told not to marry or have children in the land (16:2-3). But this was another cost Jeremiah would have to pay in the process of serving Him. That might seem to be an unreasonable requirement for God to make; yet we accept by faith that no obligation God places on us is against our own interest. As God goes on to explain, the situation in the land would become so horrifying that the burden of family would create more hardships and challenges than it would alleviate.

God's request is not without precedent in Scripture. Paul says something similar in 1 Corinthians 7, although he does not give an absolute requirement. The situation in Corinth would soon reach the point that they would consider marriage to be a burden. Perhaps governmental pressure would force a man to choose between his faith and the welfare of his family. Similar forces had compelled Paul himself to remain unmarried.

Not too long after Jeremiah was told to refrain from marriage, Ezekiel lost his own wife. In Ezekiel 25:15-17, the prophet's wife is taken from him as part of the message he was to give to the exiles in Babylonia. Not only did she die with only a few hours' notice, Ezekiel was specifically prohibited from going through the usual rites of mourning. This would tell the exiles that the woes they were enduring were a just and righteous punishment from God, not to be mourned.

Jeremiah's loss, too, carried with it a message of justice and punishment. Mourning was inappropriate under the circumstances (16:5-9). There would be no cause for rejoicing in the coming days, as the Babylonians and the disaster they brought came closer and closer to Jerusalem.

But the disaster, though not quickly done, would eventually pass. Even the greatness of the nation's deliverance from Egypt would fade in comparison to the return from Babylon that the next generation would experience (16:14-15). After having been scattered to the four winds, God brings them home. He likens it to sending fishermen out to find fish, or hunters to find game (16:16-18). After they had properly suffered for their crimes, God would bring them home again.

How does the wrath of God teach the power, might and "name" of the Lord (16:21)?

_____

_____

Jeremiah's Story:
The Men of Anathoth

People who have godly values, who try to spend quality time around others who think the same, can be in for a rude awakening when they realize how vicious people can be – including people they once considered close friends. Jeremiah appears to have had no idea about the plots against him until God revealed it to him (11:18-19). It is easy, and perhaps not a bad thing, to be idealistic about people – especially the people of God. But we should always remember that, although God will never fail us, His people sometimes will. This is particularly the case when we have a message from God that our friends do not care to hear.

In Jeremiah's case, he was telling them about the sin in the nation – and in his friends' own lives, it would appear from their reaction. And they were willing to go to great extremes to keep Jeremiah from preaching it anymore.

Will our friends be more likely to listen to condemnation from the Gospel if we are the ones giving it? _____
_____
_____

It might seem on the surface that Jeremiah took the opposition of his friends personally, and perhaps he did. It is easy to think that people's response to the message we bring from God is all about us, when in reality it is primarily about their response to God. Still, it hurts. We want vindication from God, a demonstration that we are right and our opponents are wrong. And we want to see it with our own eyes (11:20). But it is His vengeance ultimately, not our own. We wait for Him to work His righteousness in His way and His time. The commitment we have made to His cause will be shown to be the right choice; we just have to continue in faith while we wait.

What is the difference between His vengeance and our own? _____
_____
_____

Jeremiah's confidence in God was well placed. God promised him that punishment was coming for these rebellious and irreverent ones. Sword and famine were coming to them, and – unlike the fate of the nation as a whole – a remnant would not be left of them to carry on (11:22-23).

Did God say Jeremiah's life would improve right away? _____
_____
_____

Key Image: Doubly Repay (16:18)

In modern English, the idea of "doubly repaying" a grievance would probably mean to get twice as much revenge as there was infraction in the first place. But we must remember, the Bible was not written in modern English. Words, and particularly figures of speech, translated literally may not give a proper account of what the Bible is trying to say. As always, the best way to understand such things is to examine the context – and that means the context of the passage, the book, the culture, and the Bible as a whole.

Since the idea of God giving us twice as much punishment as our sins deserve is by definition unfair, and probably impossible, we are compelled to look for a figurative meaning. Looking at the way the phrase is used elsewhere in the text, it seems fair to say "doubly repay" is a figure of speech that should be interpreted as "pay back exactly what is appropriate." The language comes from a time when two-pan scales would be used in business transactions. A purchase would be placed in one side of the scale, and the weight of the amount of goods being purchased would go in the other. The weight in the scale would thus be "doubled," creating a fair transaction. Revelation 18:6-7 is a useful commentary. In this text – written by a Jewish man, using a great deal of the same figurative language found in the Old Testament – paying back double is synonymous with "to the degree."

God does not cause us to pay for our sins twice – as though we could spend two eternities in hell. He punishes to the degree that, in His wisdom, He finds appropriate, and then He stops (Isaiah 40:2).

Key Image: "Those Destined for ..." (15:2)

Throughout the Old and New Testaments, God has indicated that He has a plan for mankind – a plan for the faithful, and a plan for the rebellious. Some translations call this being "predestined," others use "foreordained." It doesn't mean people do not have free will; it means God has predetermined from long ago what will happen to us, depending on which of the two camps we fall. Through Jeremiah He is emphasizing that the people have chosen their own destiny. Some may fall in this way or that way, but all will fall. No one can stop the plan of God that has been in motion since time began.

Had the nation chosen a different path, it would have received a different "destiny." Indeed, God put His righteous wrath away many times with the unrighteous nation. But His mercy only brought on further and deeper rebellion. At this point there was nothing Jeremiah or anyone else could do to stave off the inevitable.

Key Verse: Jeremiah 12:15

If you have run with footmen and they have tired you out, then how can you compete with horses? If you fall down in a land of peace, how will you do in the thicket of the Jordan?

Key Lessons

- *Hard times should cause us to look to God:* Whether He brings relief or not, we will be blessed.
- *There is no point in arguing with God:* Far better to get used to bad news than to invent good news.
- *Short-term suffering and joy are meaningless in the big picture:* Our relationship with God is all that truly matters.

Lesson 5
Rejection
Jeremiah 17 - 23

No man likes to be turned down by the woman he loves in favor of another man. And God loves His people far more than any human loves anyone or anything; He is love embodied (1 John 4:8). But God's mourning over His lost love would not be done in silence. The rejection He felt from Judah's continued involvement with idols would be met harshly, and with little delay.

Rejecting the Inheritance

Most people are eager to receive a blessing from a loved one who has passed, assuming the bequest is something of intrinsic or personal value. And God had given Judah exactly what she had wanted – security, stability, ample blessings. But instead of praising God for these things, Judah did what her errant sister to the north had done – taken them for granted, attributed them to their own strength and cunning, and sought the favor of other nations in order to preserve them. In so doing, they revoked the terms of God's will, as it were; they rejected the terms of their inheritance and were to be stripped of it (17:4). It is much like a parent who is forced to follow through with a threat delivered to a child; "I am not taking your privileges away," the parent might say, "you took them away yourself with your poor choices." They could have trusted in God for their future; instead they trusted flawed mankind (17:5). They could have dwelled in the land God had prepared for them; instead they chose exile in the wilderness (17:6). They could have been like the "tree planted by the water" (17:7-8), an image borrowed from Psalm 1. They could have been constantly nourished and refreshed by a God who truly wanted them to succeed. But they chose to go a different path.

A decision like that seems hopelessly delusional. Why would someone do such a thing? God gives the answer; it comes from trusting in one's own deceitful heart instead of in God (17:9-10). He tests us and knows our true values, our true intentions. He knows how we can delude ourselves into thinking we can go our own way without penalty, and even prosper in doing so. Surely the heart has gotten no more astute in our day; surely we would do well to reject what we "feel" about a matter in favor of what God has revealed.

In what ways might we put our trust in mankind instead of God? _____
_____
_____

Profaning the Sabbath

From even before the giving of the Ten Commandments, Israel was required to keep the sabbath (Exodus 16:22-26). When manna was withheld on the sabbath after coming in double quantity the day before, Israel was being taught that God would provide for them even if they dedicated one day in the week wholly to Him. Extra work was a sign of a lack of trust in the One who provides. Evidently by Jeremiah's day, the sabbath was being largely ignored – at least in terms of commerce. Jeremiah warned kings and citizens alike to not bring loads through the city gates on the sabbath (17:21-22). Israel had violated the first sabbath, and no doubt many other sabbaths had been violated as well (17:23).

God required the people to accept His word that they would prosper more by trusting in Him than by working an extra day in the week. If they would do so, kings would continue to reign in Jerusalem and the city would remain habited perpetually (17:24-26). The nation could still be preserved. The line of David could remain on the throne. But continuing to abuse the sabbath would mean bringing the wrath of God down upon the nation. The very stability they were trying to ensure with extra work would be taken away.

In what way or ways do we keep the principles of the sabbath day today? _____
_____
_____

The Potter's House

A trip to the potter's house gave Jeremiah a lesson in divine sovereignty that still resonates with us today. As Jeremiah watched, the potter's creation became spoiled; the potter responded by starting over again with a new plan and a new vessel (18:1-4). God's lesson to Jeremiah, and by extension to us, is that God has the right to have certain expectations of His creation – and that, in the event that the creation fails to live up to those expectations, He has the right to dispose of it as He sees fit and start anew (18:5-6). That had applications to the rise of Babylon and its role in judgment against Judah, as well as the fortunes of Judah itself. God is in charge of rising and falling empires; they do so at His command and according to His wisdom (18:7-10). The nations themselves have as little to say in the matter as the clay has on the potter's wheel.

As is typically the case, God's warnings are also calls to repentance (18:11). It was not too late for the clay to submit to the potter. God was determined to create in Judah a vessel for His glory, and time still remained for Judah to make it so. But just as the potter's control over the clay is limited, so also the God of heaven will yield to the will of His rebellious people if they are determined to reject Him. And such was the case in Jeremiah's day. Further preaching from Jeremiah was "hopeless"; they had chosen stubbornness and an evil heart over God's righteousness (18:12). It is doubtful that these were the exact words of the people to whom Jeremiah spoke, but they may as well have been; this was their attitude, and it was for this that God would judge them. As unthinkable as it may have been for God's people to reject Him – as unthinkable as snow not falling on the mountaintops and melting into cold, refreshing water in the spring – still that is exactly what Judah had chosen to do (18:13-14).

But then, as though their moral position was not compromised enough, the people took their anger out on Jeremiah. His prophecies were simply unthinkable; they must be false, and He must be stopped (18:18). Quickly Jeremiah became aware of the talk and turned to God for support (18:19-20). Essentially he did exactly what Judah would not: when serving God left questions unanswered and problems unsolved, he dug deep and trusted in God that much more. That is the difference between faith and faithlessness.

Is our assessment of our own righteousness valid? _____
_____
_____

A Request from Zedekiah

The prophecy of Jeremiah 21 appears to have been given during the final siege of Jerusalem; the city was besieged only once during Zedekiah's time on the throne, and we read of siege engines standing outside the city walls as the prophecy was given (21:4). Zedekiah, ruling in the place of his nephew, Jehoshaphat, sent to Jeremiah to inquire as to whether God might show mercy (21:1-2). If it seems like Zedekiah's effort might fall under the heading of "too little, too late," it seems God would agree with you. The time had long passed for the king of Judah to lead the nation in national repentance and submission to the will of God, and in so doing perhaps turn away some part of God's wrath. Now, instead of turning Babylon back, God would turn back Zedekiah's feeble efforts at rebellion.

The message from Jeremiah was simply more of what he had delivered in recent years: pestilence, famine, sword and capture (21:5-7; 15:2). The mind of the people had not changed; the will of God had not changed; the attitude of the king had not changed; why would the future change? Jeremiah pleaded with Zedekiah, much as Moses had with the people in the last days of the wilderness wanderings (Deuteronomy 30:19-20), to choose life over death (Jeremiah 21:8-10). Surrender would be more than a humiliation; it would in effect trust an evil, bloodthirsty warlord to show mercy when he would have little reason to do so. But God, through Jeremiah, said that trusting in Babylon would be the same as trusting in Him. Again, the people and the king were asked to accept an uncomfortable truth and do a distasteful task to show their faith; again, tragically, they failed to do so.

What circumstances might arise in which we might be forced to "take our medicine" for sin? _____
_____
_____

The Family of Josiah

It seems unthinkable that none of the three sons of Josiah shared his faith. As righteous as Josiah was, Jehoahaz, Jehoiakim and Zedekiah were equally determined to subvert and ignore the will of God. First came "Shallum," as Jehoahaz is termed here (22:11-12). His three short months on the throne ended in disgrace and would culminate, Jeremiah said, in death while still captive in Egypt. Then came Jehoiakim, who quickly showed himself to be more interested in building himself a large house of cedar than a culture of reform as his father had done (22:13-17). His fate would be as ignominious as his reign – "buried with a donkey's burial, dragged off and thrown out beyond the gates of Jerusalem" (22:19).

Jehoiachin, the son of Jehoiakim who would follow him on the throne, would be no better in his short reign. Jehoiachin would show himself to be his father's son. As a result, he and the line of David are cursed by God. The young "Coniah" (22:24-30) would never see his son arise to the throne. Instead he would yield the throne to his uncle, Zedekiah, who would be witness to the final destruction of Judah and Jerusalem.

What implication does this have for the reign of Jesus, who was descended from Coniah (Matthew 1:1, 11)? _____
_____
_____

Jeremiah's Story:
In the Stocks

God never said preaching His message would be easy. Jeremiah, if he did not know this already, found out after he preached the message of the broken jar. At God's command, he shattered an earthenware vessel in the sight of all, saying the nation's destruction would be every bit as irreparable (19:1-11). Topheth in the valley of Ben-Hinnom, where Josiah had once taken a firm stand against idolatry (2 Kings 23:10), would be the site of tremendous slaughter; the victims would be buried where they fell, evidently because the proper graveyards would be full already (19:11).

What are "stiff-necked" people unable to do (19:15)? _____

_____

_____

Jeremiah's message found its target audience, and the reaction was not pretty. Pashhur the priest, "chief officer in the house of the LORD" (20:1), had Jeremiah left in stocks overnight directly adjacent to the temple of the God Jeremiah was serving and Pashhur was rejecting (20:2). Pashhur appears to be a different man from "Pashhur the son of Malchijah" who petitioned Jeremiah on behalf of Zedekiah later (21:1-2).

Why would Pashhur respond so violently? _____

_____

_____

Immediately upon being released from the stocks, Jeremiah lashed out against his oppressor. Pashhur would be known prophetically as Magor-missabib, which is translated "terror on every side." Pashhur's own life would come to reflect everything that was terrifying about the coming days. He would survive to see the truth of Jeremiah's prophecies, watching as the friends who had trusted in his words fell by the sword (20:3-4). Pashhur himself would go with his family to Babylon, where he would die and be buried (2:6).

In what way would Pashhur be a "terror" to himself and others? _____

_____

_____

Key Image: The Righteous Branch (23:5)

The prophets speak repeatedly of a character called "the Branch" (Jeremiah 33:15-16; Isaiah 4:2; Zechariah 3:8, 6:12-13). This One is said to bring the reign of David back to Israel, but in a spiritual way. These passages foretell of Jesus, who would come to bring the prophecy of 2 Samuel 7:12-13 to its full and spiritual fulfillment. It is He who would unite the people of God under one Head and lead them in righteous paths.

Similar language is seen in Isaiah 11:1. He would shoot forth from the root or stem of Jesse, indicating sudden life coming from lifelessness. When all hope for the nation was lost, a King would arise that would bring the people of God to a place far greater than they had ever known, even under David.

Several of these texts specifically emphasize the reunion of Israel and Judah and the renewed offering of proper sacrifices – an issue the righteous souls of Jeremiah's day could not help but appreciate. The spiritual kingdom of Jesus provides for all saints to be priests (Revelation 1:6), joining together as His spiritual body to form a spiritual temple in which proper sacrifices of the heart would continue as long as the body remains (1 Peter 2:4-5). Key image: "Is not my word like fire?" (23:29)

God's word is powerful; its impact can be ignored as much as a rock can ignore the hammer that smashes it into bits. When the two disciples on the Emmaus road realized they had been in the presence of Jesus, they chided themselves for not realizing sooner; "Were not our hearts burning within us while He was speaking to us on the road, while He was explaining the Scriptures to us?" they ask in Luke 24:32. That is what the true word of God does when it finds an ear to hear.

God's word could not be more dissimilar to the words spoken in His name by presumptive prophets. He compares it to the difference between worthless straw and nutritious grain (23:28). They might call them "dreams," but that did not make them from God. And those who followed after the dreams instead of the true teachings of God revealed through Jeremiah could not possibly reap the benefits they sought (23:32). You cannot draw closer to God by following words that do not come from God.

Key Verse: Jeremiah 20:9

But if I say, "I will not remember Him or speak anymore in His name," then in my heart it becomes like a burning fire shut up in my bones; and I am weary of holding it in, and I cannot endure it.

Key Lessons

- *God communicates His will*. Whether we listen is up to us.
- *Opposing God's people equates to opposing God*. God will not allow offenses against His faithful to go unavenged.
- *The line of David in Jerusalem is over*. The succession of kings would end with Jehoiachin (Coniah).

Lesson 6
Captivity
Jeremiah 24 - 28

Israelite history is littered with stories of foreign oppressors. Whether Philistines in David's day, Midianites in Gideon's day, Arameans in Elisha's day, or any number of other examples which could be mentioned, the cause for such invasions, occupations and subjugations was consistent: idolatry. When the nation refused to honor God as the first commandment required, the nation suffered – and sometimes, suffered mightily. But what lay in store for Judah in Jeremiah's day was different.

The Fall of Jerusalem

It takes about as long to sort through all of Jehoiachin's names and nicknames as he lasted on the throne in Jerusalem. Often called Jeconiah or Coniah in Jeremiah's prophecy (24:1), the son of Jehoiakim was king for just three months before Nebuchadnezzar came to Jerusalem and took him, along with 10,000 other captives back to Babylon (2 Kings 24:8-16). The natural assumption, both for the exiles in Babylonia and for those left behind in Jerusalem, was that the exiles were receiving the brunt of God's wrath. In fact, it was just the opposite – God had removed Jeconiah, Ezekiel and the rest so as to spare them the worst of the consequences, which was yet to come.

Jeremiah was given a vision of two baskets of figs – one fresh, one rotten. They represented the people of God, at home and in exile, and their respective spiritual states. But it was the exiles who were the "good figs" (24:5). They would be blessed in exile and ultimately returned to repopulate the land. The "bad figs which cannot be eaten due to rottenness" represented Zedekiah and those left behind in Jerusalem (24:8-10). What might have seemed like a blessing would turn out, as years progressed, to be a terrible curse.

Was it fair for Jeremiah to stay behind and suffer along with the dregs of society? ___
_____
_____

The 70 Years

Jeremiah had been preaching the same message of repentance for 23 years by the time Jehoiakim reached his fourth year on the throne (25:1-4). If the people would turn back to God, they would be spared the brunt of His wrath at the hands of the Babylonians. If they continued to rebel, their fate would only worsen. It appears 23 years was enough. Through Jeremiah God announced that the hostilities of the day would be resolved, in Babylon's favor, as He had long promised they would be.

Beginning in that year, thought to be 609 B.C., Judah would be a vassal state of Babylon. For 70 years they would serve their foreign masters (25:8-11). But in the end, they would be allowed to return. For Babylon itself, on the other hand, complete destruction lay ahead. The words of condemnation written by Jeremiah and other prophets had not been forgotten; they, too, were promises of God that would be fulfilled after 70 years (25:13-14).

How would Judah be "a horror and a hissing?" _____

_____

_____

The Cup of God's Wrath

Drunkenness is a common metaphor in the Bible. Typically it refers to a state of one's own choosing that drives one further and further away from God's plan for one's life. Once drunkenness is realized and the symptoms start to manifest themselves, the drinker may regret the path he has chosen; but by this time it is too late, and he must deal with the bed he has made for himself.

Such is the case when the nations, particularly Babylon, were required to drink the "cup of the wine of wrath" (25:15). Like a literal drunk, these nations "stagger and go mad" because of the fate God had in store for them (25:16). And if perchance they, like Pharaoh in days of old, gave an indication that perhaps they would rather choose sobriety, God would force them to drink (25:25-29). Half-hearted repentance will not be accepted on that day. God chose a fate for them, and that fate will be delivered in full. The same fate is in store for all wicked nations – and all wicked people as well. Doom may be delayed through God's mercy and patience, but that does not make it any less real or certain. The inhabitants of the earth, all of them, are accountable to God and subject to His wrath when they do not submit to Him (25:30-38).

Why would drunkenness be used as a symbol of God's wrath? _____

_____

_____

Prophet vs. Prophet

Jeremiah was by no means the only prophet of God in the land at that time. Several references are made to others. But being a prophet – or perhaps more accurately, calling oneself a prophet – did not give any assurance of accuracy or validity. This is clearly seen in the exchange between Jeremiah and Hananiah. After Jeremiah preached in a yoke in chapter 27, indicating graphically the "yoke" of Babylonian subjection Judah would wear, Hananiah intervened to specifically contradict Jeremiah. Yes, clearly, the yoke was there; already the sacred vessels of the temple had been removed along with the king and 10,000 other captives; but all of it would be reversed in two years (28:2-4) – not 70, as Jeremiah had said.

Jeremiah's response was classic: "Amen! May the LORD do so; may the LORD confirm your words which you have prophesied to bring back the vessels of the LORD's house and all the exiles, from Babylon to this place" (28:6). After all, who wouldn't want such a prophecy to come true? But clearly Jeremiah is speaking a bit tongue-in-cheek; he immediately followed up his "approval" with a warning, echoing the test of a prophet given in Deuteronomy 18:22 – the true prophet was the one whose prophecies actually came true (28:7-9).

Hananiah appeared to have taken Jeremiah's words poorly. He took Jeremiah's yoke and broke it in front of all, further emphasizing the breaking of Babylonian bondage. Of course,

Hananiah was free to speculate about the future, to accept Jeremiah's words or reject them, as are we all. What made Hananiah's actions different was, he invoked the name of God; and then he did it again (28:2, 10). These were not Hananiah's own personal speculations; this was the word of God Almighty Himself – according to Hananiah, at least.

As Hananiah escalated the rhetoric, so did Jeremiah. The wooden yoke would only be replaced by one of iron – a stronger, more durable, and probably more painful one (28:13). And beyond that, Hananiah himself was told that he would die that very year because of his presumption. And he did (28:15-17). We can only imagine the reaction as the people watched the words of Jeremiah fulfilled in their eyes. Any reasonable observer would be able to see the answer to the question of which prophet truly spoke for God. If Jeremiah was right about Hananiah dying, surely that would mean that Jeremiah's words about the captivity, and not Hananiah's, would be correct as well.

How did Hananiah counsel "rebellion against the LORD?" _____

_____

_____

Jeremiah's Story:
The Death Sentence

Jeremiah was a public figure by the time Jehoiakim assumed the throne. Considering the change of kings that had taken place, along with the fact that Jehoiakim had originally been passed over in favor of his younger brother (2 Kings 23:31-36), it was reasonable to think the people would have liked to hear from Jeremiah – and by extension, from God – about the state of affairs and the direction of the nation. But Jeremiah's message was not a pleasant one; he said the same thing he had been saying for years. Repent of sin. Accept God's chastening. Remember times of destruction that occurred before (26:4-6).

Was it possible for the people to repent at this stage? _____

_____

_____

To put the reaction of Jeremiah's detractors in perspective (and not justify them in any way), when people are told to abandon their nation and throw themselves on the mercy of foreign oppressors, they frequently respond badly. And the priests and prophets – perhaps offended personally, perhaps wanting to make a good impression on the new king – certainly took great umbrage at Jeremiah's words. In fact, they considered his words a killing offense (26:7-9).

Why was prophesying against Jerusalem so objectionable? _____

_____

_____

Unafraid, Jeremiah repeated his message when called to account for himself before the officials of Judah (26:10-13). He was willing, much like the three exiles from Judah who faced the fiery furnace a few years later (Daniel 3:16-18), to accept the fate that would be determined for him. However, he insisted he was innocent of any crimes against God or the nation, and the price of shedding innocent blood would be theirs to pay (26:14-15).

But at that point, the spirit of the crowd turned. The officials and the people showed respect for Jeremiah, since he had spoken "in the name of the LORD our God" (26:16). God's name still carried weight, even in the nation that was busy about the task of abandoning Him. And some elders appealed to Micah's prophecy a century before which had been preserved and studied, which had spoken of Zion being "plowed as a field" (26:17-19; Micah 3:12). Perhaps Ahikam was one of the voices of reason on that day (26:24); in any case, Jeremiah's life was spared.

Not everyone got such reasoned justice, though. Jehoiakim chased another prophet, Uriah the son of Shemaiah, all the way to Egypt, took him captive, slew him, and cast him into an unmarked common grave (26:20-23).

Why did the officials spare Jeremiah's life? _____

_____

_____

Key image: Seventy Years (25:11-12)

Numbers often have symbolic meaning, particularly in the Bible. Seven often denotes completeness or perfection. John records in his gospel account seven signs done by Jesus to completely prove His divine nature. Seven churches in Asia describe the entire body of Christ in Revelation 2-3. Ten is a power number; multiples of ten are used for emphasis, as with the "myriads of myriads, and thousands of thousands" before the throne in Revelation 5:11. Therefore 70 could be seen as having symbolic value beyond the literal duration of Judah's time in Babylonia.

There is also 2 Chronicles 36:20-21, which indicates that the "sabbaths" for the land required in Leviticus 25:4 may have been ignored. If it had been 490 years since the sabbath of the land was properly observed (many date the conquest of Canaan at around 1280 B.C.), it may have been a way of God emphasizing the protracted pattern of rebellion among His people. In any event, allowing the land a sabbath rest is specifically mentioned in Leviticus 26:34-35 as a punishment for national disobedience. The land was intended to be a blessing to the people; if they refused to properly honor God, He would refuse to bless them.

Key Image: Everlasting Destruction (25:9, 12)

Words define themselves in context. The meanings we place upon them because of our own usage and experience may not be what God had intended. "Everlasting desolation" is an example. We might think that it implies a destruction that never ends, or persists into eternity. But the context shows us clearly that "everlasting" has more to do with the degree of punishment than the duration.

The same "everlasting desolation" promised to Judah and the nations punished by Babylon was promised for Babylon itself. But Judah would be rebuilt; Babylon would not. The Bible uses the word "forever" similarly: flawed humans perish forever (Job 4:20); God would reject Solomon forever if he abandoned God (1 Chronicles 28:9); the wicked would be broken down forever (Psalm 52:5), etc. The point is to emphasize the magnitude and lingering memory of the destruction, not its literal duration.

Key Verse: Jeremiah 24:7

I will give them a heart to know Me, for I am the LORD; and they will be My people, and I will be their God, for they will return to Me with their whole heart.

Key Lessons

- *Righteousness is no guarantee of safety.* Even godly souls may be asked to pay a steep price.
- *God puts nations and people in power as He sees fit.* God rules, not Nebuchadnezzar or any earthly king.
- *A prophet is as a prophet does.* Those who speak words that do not come true are to be rejected.

Lesson 7
Covenant
Jeremiah 29 - 33

A covenant is a bargain between two consenting parties. God offered the covenant to Abraham in varying stages dating back even to his days in Ur and Haran. Ultimately he was promised great blessings in the land and in his family. But the faith of Abraham was not always found in his descendants. God made clear, particularly when the covenant was reiterated through Moses, that He would not fulfil his part of the covenant if Israel was unfaithful in its part. When the people were found in violation, they were chastened. Now God was prepared to revoke His part of the covenant in a manner the people would never have imagined, although He had given them ample warning to that effect.

A Letter to the Exiles

Shortly after the fall of Jerusalem, Jeremiah sent a letter to his exiled brethren. The text is unclear how frequent or detailed communication was between Jeremiah and the exiles. It is possible that word got back to Jeremiah about the state of affairs in Babylonia through conventional channels. It is also possible that God simply revealed the truth to Jeremiah directly; if this was the case, Jeremiah's words should have carried more weight with his audience. But however it happened, Jeremiah became informed of false prophets among the exiles, and God inspired him to rebuke them. He encouraged the exiles to live normal lives in their new surroundings (29:4-9). They were not leaving anytime soon. However, he promised, the nation would have opportunity to return to Jerusalem and Judah after the appointed 70 years of captivity were concluded (29:10). As horrific as the immediate bad news was, good news loomed on the horizon; God had "a future and a hope" in mind for His people (29:11).

The news was not good, however, for the false prophets. Ahab and Zedekiah, guilty of speaking falsely in God's name, would be destroyed in such a way as to become a warning to all who would follow. Nebuchadnezzar, who either already knew about their subversive talk or became aware of it after Jeremiah's letter (29:3), was going to bring them to a sudden and horrific end. The language indicating they were "roasted in the fire" may not be figurative; Nebuchadnezzar dealt with at least some rebellious elements in just such a way (Daniel 3:6), and it is more than likely that Ahab and Zedekiah were consigned to the same fiery end as were Shadrach, Meshech and Abed-nego – minus the supernatural preservation of life, obviously.

Does God have "a future and a hope" for us? _____

_____

_____

The Politics of Shemaiah

The false prophets were not satisfied with stirring up local discontent, though. Shemaiah the Nehelamite had written to allies back in Jerusalem suggesting that God wanted Zephaniah (apparently the brother of the false prophet Zedekiah) to usurp Jehoiada's role as priest, and then use his new power to silence "every madman who prophesies, to put him in the stocks and in the iron collar" (29:24-28) – a thinly veiled reference to Jeremiah himself. When Jeremiah heard of this, Shemaiah's name was added to the list of unfaithful "prophets"; he and his family would not live to see the revival of the nation of which Jeremiah had spoken (29:32).

Why did Shemaiah feel he could succeed in his efforts to undermine Jeremiah? _____
_____
_____

The Book of Consolation

It is remarkable that just as the news in Jerusalem could not get any worse, Jeremiah's prophecy takes a turn for the positive. It was becoming increasingly impossible to deny the reality of the situation, not only for the present but also for the foreseeable future. Everything else Jeremiah had said about the nation had come true; no doubt people were starting to believe the prophecy of 70 years in captivity would be true as well. At this point, when all seemed lost, God gave a special word to Jeremiah and told him to write it in a book (30:2). Of course, many or perhaps even all of Jeremiah's other prophecies eventually found their way into a book as well; this small section, though, seems to have been special. Perhaps it was circulated among the besieged people and eventually the exiles even before the rest. Scholars have taken to calling chapters 30-33 of our text "the Book of Consolation." and it comprises visions and anecdotes from the final days of Zedekiah's reign in Jerusalem. Despite appearances, God had not abandoned His people; these words were intended to give them comfort while they waited for His mercy (30:1-3).

The distress they faced was real, no doubt; and it would only get worse (30:5-7). But, as is often the case when childbirth is the metaphor, the extreme pain would be followed shortly by great joy. A rejuvenated nation would emerge from the ashes, under the headship of "the LORD their God and David their king" (30:8-9). Since David himself was long dead, not to return (Acts 2:29), and his family line ended with Jeconiah (22:30), "David" is a figurative name. The reunion of "My people Israel and Judah" (30:3) refers to the spiritual conjoining of all people of faith from all corners of the earth, all ethnicities, all native tongues. "David" is a name for the Messiah to come (Ezekiel 34:23-24, 37:24-25; Hosea 3:5), much like "Immanuel" (Isaiah 7:14) and "Wonderful Counselor, Mighty God, Eternal Father, Prince of Peace" (Isaiah 9:6). The name given to Messiah gives insight into what sort of king He would be.

What similarities exist between David and Jesus? _____
_____
_____

Type and Antitype

Type-antitype imagery is common in the Bible. The "type" is the shadow, the foretaste of what is to come. The "antitype" is the greater reality, the substance which gives extra meaning to the message sent before by the "type." Frequently the relationship between the two is only seen in retrospect; only by looking back at the figures in the Old Testament in the context of their fulfillment in the New Testament can we properly understand the eternal plan of God as it was spelled out in mystery over the centuries.

The return of Judah to Jerusalem is classic type-antitype imagery. Yes, the nation would return to Jerusalem and be restored. But the greater message was that the downfall of the political nation of Israel would be followed by the spiritual nation arising from the ashes. All of God's people would be gathered under the leadership of "David" – not just the exiles and their descendants (30:9). No doubt the revival under Zerubbabel, Ezra and Nehemiah was partially in view when Jeremiah wrote of the restoration (30:18), and perhaps Zerubbabel himself is their "leader" (30:21). But the overall arc of the Book of Consolation requires that we see far more than just political or even spiritual restoration in this prophecy.

If we were in doubt, the prophecy regarding Rachel and her children (31:15) puts the argument to rest. Matthew 2:18 identifies this as a prophecy of the slaughter of innocents around the time of Jesus' birth in Bethlehem. The mother of Benjamin is seen as weeping over the death of her innocent descendants in the tribe of Benjamin (Joshua 18:21-28); surely the slaughter wrought by Nebuchadnezzar in Zedekiah's day was too horrible to contemplate. But, as Jeremiah emphasized, the nation would return; Rachel's weeping would eventually be replaced with tears of joy. The atrocities of Herod may have seemed even worse; how could killing innocent children in an effort to eliminate a potential political opponent still in the cradle lead to anything positive? Yet this is precisely the wondrous resolution God accomplished in the life of Jesus, beginning in those early days and weeks in Bethlehem.

This new nation, though, would cling to her spiritual Husband more faithfully than had been the case previously. Roadmarks and guideposts were to be set up ahead of time, before they were forced to abandon the Promised Land, so that the next generation could find its way home (31:21). Only by trusting in the "ancient paths" long since abandoned (6:16) could the new nation "encompass" God with love and devotion (31:22). And of course, the same principles apply to the church; by adhering to the faith of Abraham (Romans 4:1-13), we can find a truly loving and fruitful relationship with our Creator

Should thoughts of a secure future in God give us pleasant sleep (31:26)? Why might it not? _____

_____

_____

_____

"A New Covenant"

It seems the people of Jeremiah's day had convinced themselves they were being punished solely for the actions of previous generations; "the fathers have eaten sour grapes, and the children's teeth are set on edge" (31:29; Ezekiel 18:2). Hopefully, through the work of Jeremiah and Ezekiel, they would come to realize their own responsibility. If they did, and became the chastened remnant God had in mind, they would be freed to start over again with their Heavenly Father.

The idea of a fresh start in that day prefigures the "new covenant" (31:31) that would be established in Jesus. Through Jesus the people would have the law "within them ... on their heart" (31:33). Their relationship would be personal and not national; one would have to "know the LORD" to become part of His people in the first place (31:34). Most significantly, being found in Jesus would mean true forgiveness of sins (31:34).

Such a reality might be too much for the bedraggled upstarts of Zedekiah's Jerusalem to accept. But Jeremiah reminds them that the same God who "gives the sun for light by day and the fixed order of the moon and the stars for light by night" is giving them this promise; if He is found faithful in the one, they can trust Him to be faithful in the other (31:35-37).

How is the citizen of Jesus' kingdom different from a descendant of Abraham under the Law of Moses? _____

_____

_____

Jeremiah's Story:
Buying a Field

In the throes of the siege, Zedekiah managed to find time to visit Jeremiah in prison. Even at this late stage, the king could not understand why Jeremiah had to be so negative all the time. Clearly Zedekiah had been listening; he recited Jeremiah's main talking points about as well as Jeremiah had (32:2-5). It made no sense to him that the prophet would persist in bringing this message of doom. Jeremiah's response was, no doubt, unexpected: he told the king about the day God spoke to him and told him to buy real estate.

How did Jeremiah's response answer Zedekiah's question? _____

_____

_____

The market for land had never been worse; the forests had been stripped for siege engines, the fields were ransacked, and soon the city itself would fall. And this was the time that Jeremiah's near relative Hanamel would come and offer Jeremiah the "opportunity" to buy some family property. God told Jeremiah that Hanamel would make the offer – and that Jeremiah should accept it. In the ancient equivalent of "putting your money where your mouth is," Jeremiah's confidence in the return and rise of Judah became a matter of public record. Yes, things were horrible. But they would get better. "Houses and fields and vineyards will again be bought in this land," he said (32:15). And the God who gave him the message, the one for whom nothing is too difficult (32:17, 27), would surely be true to His word.

Who is able to find comfort in this sort of message? _____

_____

_____

As usual, the words of God were difficult to swallow. As hard as it was to believe God would allow His people to be taken into captivity, it was even harder to imagine them coming back from it. But just as the cause of His wrath was real (32:31-35), so also would be His mercy in the end. The power of the king of Babylon was no match for the power of the One who gave him the power in the first place. If God was determined to bring His people home and establish "an everlasting covenant with them" (32:40), nothing could stand in His way.

What might be considered a barrier between us and heaven? Can God overcome such things? _____

_____

_____

Key Image: The Heart (29:13)

Even today, the "heart" often has reference to something other than the large muscle that pumps blood throughout the body. Generally, what a person is said to be "in his heart" or "on the inside" is meant to depict his true self. Thus we are to love God with our whole heart (Matthew 22:37; Deuteronomy 6:5). Judah had not done that. Although the people had been willing to offer God part of their loyalty, they reserved part for their idols.

True repentance begins in the heart. We must truly want to pursue the things of God from the inside out. The ones who are truly the people of God are willing and eager to do that (24:7). But even then, we can find His way for us only by searching with our whole heart, truly devoting ourselves to Him.

Key Image: Latter Days (30:24)

The term "latter days" or "last days" occurs many times in both Old and New Testaments. Perhaps the first impulse is to assume that they refer to "end-time events" – that is, the end of the world and the return of Christ. But that is not true to the usage of the terms in Scripture. They simply mean days that are still to come, days that have not yet arrived. Peter (2 Peter 3:3) and Paul (1 Timothy 4:1) use the idea to convey the fulfillment of specific prophecy given in the First Century – prophecy that was, at least in part, fulfilled in the First Century (Jude 17-19). Likewise, in Hebrews 1:2, "these last days" refers to the gospel era, "days" that were currently being lived in by the Christians of that day.

The length or purpose of our wait for these "days," whether they are specific warnings for modern readers, whether the days may have in fact arrived between the time of writing and the time of reading – these are issues that must be resolved in the context of each individual appearance.

Key Verse: Jeremiah 32:27

Behold, I am the LORD, the God of all flesh; is anything too difficult for Me?

Key Lessons

- *There is hope in God.* No circumstance can arise that can defeat God's plan for our lives.
- *God establishes a covenant with us in Jesus.* As with the old, those who wish to be the people of God must submit in faith.
- *There will always be a King and priests for the people of God.* Jesus reigns, and His people serve at God's altar.

Lesson 8
Obedience
Jeremiah 34 - 36

It is never too late to obey, nor is it ever too late to begin reaping the rewards of obedience. True, we cannot erase years of rebellion or the consequences that they may bring. However, opportunity to return to God remains as long as breath remains.

Zedekiah and the people had opportunities to submit to God's will, as proclaimed by Jeremiah. Babylon would still conquer; the people of God would still be enslaved for 70 years. But the severity of their punishment was still to be determined.

A Message for Zedekiah

At some point during the siege of Jerusalem, God sent Jeremiah to speak to King Zedekiah. That might seem strange in and of itself, given how resistant Zedekiah had been to Jeremiah's message throughout his reign. Even so, God saw fit to give him another chance. More than that, He even softened the message. Yes, the city would still burn (34:2-3). But Zedekiah himself would survive. Unlike his brother Jehoiakim, he would die in peace and be mourned properly (34:4-5). One cannot help but think this is God's way of offering an incentive to Zedekiah to do the right thing when "the right thing" is rapidly becoming the only option. As bad a mess as Zedekiah had made of things, God assured him, he would be spared at least some indignity. He would survive his pending appointment with Nebuchadnezzar.

About the same time, Ezekiel was giving a much different picture of Zedekiah's end. He acted out the part of the king crawling through the wall like a coward in the dead of night, then finally being caught in Nebuchadnezzar's net and dragged off to die in Babylon (Ezekiel 12:12-16). The tone of Ezekiel's words fits the record of 2 Kings 25:5-7; Ezekiel's reference to Zedekiah not seeing Babylon even though he would be taken there makes sense when we consider that Zedekiah was blinded after being forced to watch his sons slaughtered. But although the two prophecies read very differently, both were fulfilled to the letter (52:9-11). Whether God would have spared Zedekiah some of his pain and suffering in the event of repentance is impossible to say; what we do know for certain is, Zedekiah had multiple opportunities to make his soul right with God, and he passed on all of them.

Why is it important to reconcile these prophecies? _____
_____
_____

The Liberation of Servants

For reasons lost to history, Zedekiah made a covenant with the people that they would free all Jewish slaves in Jerusalem (34:8-10). It is unlikely that he made this decision because Jeremiah suggested it; we have no record of a conversation to that effect, and Zedekiah had no trouble ignoring the words of the prophet in other matters. It seems more likely that this was an idea of Zedekiah's. Perhaps he thought freed men and women would fight more effectively. Perhaps he thought abiding by the Law of Moses in this matter (Exodus

21:2-11, Deuteronomy 15:12-18) would put him in good standing with God, despite his failures in other areas. In any event, the slaves were freed.

And then a remarkable thing happened. Nebuchadnezzar lifted the siege (34:22). Historians point to archaeological evidence that the siege of Jerusalem was, in fact, lifted briefly; Nebuchadnezzar redirected his forces to confront an Egyptian uprising in 588 B.C. Although the Bible does not record this as being God's response to their actions, it may well have been; more importantly, if the people freed their slaves as a gesture of faith, they certainly would have seen the relief as having come from God.

But the joy was short-lived. As soon as the siege lifted, the people took their slaves back (34:11). Whatever commitment they had made, either to God or to human dignity, was as shallow as their "repentance" had been at various times throughout history.

Is there such a thing as "deathbed repentance?" _____

_____

_____

Meeting with the Rechabites

The making and keeping of vows was an ancient tradition among the Jews. The best known of the Israelite vows may be the Nazarite vow (Numbers 6:1-8). Although Samson is the only one specifically described as a Nazarite (Judges 13:5), others kept the vow as well (Amos 2:11-12). Men such as Samuel (1 Samuel 1:9-11) and John the Baptist (Luke 1:15) may have been Nazarites.

Jonadab the son of Rechab, too, may have been a Nazarite. Whatever vow it was he took, he required his sons to keep it as well. Not only were the Rechabites to abstain from grape products, they were not to farm at all; they were to live in tents instead of houses. The family of Jonadab had kept this vow, it seems, for at least four generations. Only the siege, which made living in the country impossible, compelled the Rechabites to move into Jerusalem with the rest of the people (35:6-11).

Knowing their commitment, and evidently wishing to make them an example of commitment, God asked Jeremiah to invite them to drink wine in one of the outer temple chambers (35:2). Naturally, Jaazaniah and the rest of the Rechabites refused. Jeremiah went on to use the Rechabites to condemn the rest of the nation for its infidelity. If Jonadab and the rest of his family could stay devoted to an extreme voluntary task, surely the nation could submit to God's own law. Consequently, Jeremiah assured the Rechabites that, whatever hardship might befall the nation, Jonadab's family would survive (35:19).

Do special personal commitments apart from God's commands have any value for us today? _____

_____

_____

_____

Jeremiah's Story:
The Burned Scroll

By the fifth year of Jehoiakim's reign, the message of Jeremiah had already begun to be fulfilled. The year before, he had announced that the invasion of Judah and the deportation of a few Jewish princes was only the beginning; it would be 70 years before the Babylonian hold over God's people would be lifted (25:11). Perhaps this pronouncement was what led to Jeremiah's restriction from public areas, particularly "the house of the LORD" (36:5).
In any event, God asked Jeremiah to put one particular prophecy in writing, to be read in public for all to hear. Jeremiah dictated the message to the scribe Baruch, and sent him to read in his place. Despite the resistance that had constantly been shown, Jeremiah still held out hope that people would hear, believe and repent (36:6-8).

Should Jeremiah have delivered the word himself (36:5-6)? _____
_____
_____

We don't know precisely what the message was, but we can safely guess. It certainly reso- nated with the court of Jehoiakim. When word got to the king's officials about what Baruch had been saying, they sent Jehudi to bring the scroll for them to examine for themselves. Baruch brought the scroll to them and read it to them as he had to the others (36:11-15).

Immediately upon hearing the message, the officials knew they needed to bring it to the king's attention. Perhaps this was to get Baruch and Jeremiah in trouble; however, the senti- ment expressed by some of them later (36:25) indicates they were more afraid for themselves and the nation than angry at Jeremiah. In either case, the king had to be informed. So after confirming that Baruch had taken dictation directly from the prophet of God, they took the scroll to the king. But first, indicating both their concern for Baruch and Jeremiah, and their inclination of how the king would respond, they told Baruch that he and Jeremiah should go into hiding (36:17-19).

True to their word, the officials took the scroll to Jehoiakim. Jehudi read it to him as he sat by the fire warming himself against the winter's cold (36:20-22). The text says, "When Jehudi had read three or four columns, the king cut it with a scribe's knife and threw it into the fire that was in the brazier, until all the scroll was consumed" (36:23). Perhaps this means the king was only willing to listen to part of the prophecy before destroying it all; perhaps he actually sat through the entire reading but destroyed the part of the text he had heard. Either way, the officials had time to protest his actions, and some did (36:25). But the king himself and his servants, those closest to him, "were not afraid, nor did they rend their garments" (36:24).

What purpose was served in destroying the scroll? _____
_____
_____

Jehoiakim was not done showing his contempt and anger toward Jeremiah and Baruch. He gave commandment to his own son, among others, to apprehend them, "but the LORD hid them" (26). God was not done with His workers quite yet.

The very next day, God spoke again to Jeremiah and told him to duplicate the words of the first scroll (36:28). This he did, with the help of Baruch, "and many similar words were added to them" (36:32). Additionally, Jeremiah was given words of prophecy regarding Jehoiakim himself – and since they were directed personally toward him, it is reasonable to assume either that Jeremiah would speak them in his hearing or that he would have access to them in some other way (36:29).

Jehoiakim's contempt for the word of God would not stand. Jeremiah was told, "He shall have no one to sit on the throne of David, and his dead body shall be cast out to the heat of the day and the frost of the night" (36:30). Although Jehoiakim's son Jeconiah did briefly reign after Jehoiakim's death, he was deposed in just three months – and Jeconiah's own sons never took the throne at all (22:30). Jehoiakim's own downfall would mirror that of Judah's – brutal, public, and unforgettable.

Why bother with another scroll? _____
_____
_____

Key Image: Release (34:17)

The whole point of bringing the descendants of Abraham, Isaac and Jacob out of Egyptian bondage was to deliver them into a state of freedom in the Promised Land. The idea of bringing one another back into slavery was abhorrent. But the release God had granted them had been rejected. They had chosen to go back into slavery, essentially. This mirrored the spiritual decline of the people; after having been granted the privilege of coming into the presence of the one true God and reaping the benefits of His fellowship, they had plunged back into idolatry. Therefore, if they would rather be "released" from the connection to God they seemed to find so objectionable, God would release them. The bonds that had kept the nation out of harm's way would be taken off, "freeing" them to their own destruction (34:17).

Key Image: Between The Parts of the Calf (34:18-20)

Animal sacrifices were much more involved than merely slaughtering an animal and roasting it. As with virtually any spiritual ritual, elaborate ceremony was often involved. Historical records and archaeological discoveries support the notion that a person in the ancient Near East would literally walk through an animal while it was being cut in half for the purpose of sacrifice. Abraham, known in his early life as Abram, was brought up in Ur of the Chaldees – which is to say, ancient Babylonia. Genesis 15:1-11 describes how he saw a vision of God (evidently in human form) and was moved to make a sacrifice to Him of several animals. The larger animals were cut in two; the birds (too small for such a gesture) were not. On this occasion God reaffirms His covenant with Abram for the first time in the land of Canaan.

Jeremiah 34:18-20 indicates the covenant imagery still remained in the slaughter of animals for sacrifice. By passing between the parts of the calf, the priest essentially became part of the sacrifice himself. It was an abomination for one who participated in the atonement for sins to flagrantly violate the covenant themselves. It was as great a defilement as allowing wild animals to feast on what was meant for God – as Abram refused to do (Genesis 15:11). Therefore, these defiled ones would be defiled themselves, left unburied as food for birds and beasts.

Key Verse: Jeremiah 36:6

So you go and read from the scroll which you have written at my dictation the words of the LORD to the people in the LORD's house on a fast day. And also you shall read them to all the people of Judah who come from their cities.

Key Lessons

- *God's people were meant to be free*: We should not be using one another as servants; we should be serving one another.
- *Honor your commitments*: Be as true to God as we are to our traditions.
- *God's word will endure*: Efforts to eliminate God's word will continue to fail.

Lesson 9
Weakness
Jeremiah 37 - 39, 52

Repeatedly in the Bible, the people of God are exhorted to be strong. God would not find it necessary to give such admonitions if weakness were not a serious problem. And it is. As much as we may be convinced that God's way is the right way, it often takes extra conviction of spirit to actually walk in it. And in the absence of His strength, we find it easier to take the path of least resistance. Resistance is low because God allows us to choose for ourselves. But just because He does not always directly intervene to force our hand does not mean He condones our weakness. We have direction from Him, we have access to it, and we have the opportunity to submit. That is all that is required for obedience. Any shortfall of character or will power that leaves us short is our fault, not His. Zedekiah found this out the hard way.

A Prayer for the Nation

The context of Jeremiah 37 indicates the siege of Jerusalem had been lifted; an uprising by the Egyptians prompted Nebuchadnezzar to break off his extended assault on Jerusalem and address more pressing matters (37:5). At this time – perhaps to confirm in his mind that God had forgiven the nation, perhaps realizing that God could easily bring the Babylonian army back – Zedekiah sent to Jeremiah, asking him to pray on behalf of the nation (37:3). His request seems ridiculous to us on multiple levels, considering the context of the book of Jeremiah and Zedekiah's own history in particular. No one had been listening to Jeremiah (37:2), including Zedekiah. And yet Jeremiah's righteousness and pathway to God was unchallenged. Perhaps Zedekiah felt unworthy to pray on his own and wanted Jeremiah to intercede on his behalf. Perhaps, from a more cynical perspective, he wanted the benefits of God's mercy without the responsibility of personal repentance and change.

God gave Jeremiah a message for Zedekiah, but it did not contain the assurances for which Zedekiah had hoped. The Chaldeans would return, God promised (37:7-10). The break was temporary. The number of soldiers amassed against Judah was immaterial; it was God, not Nebuchadnezzar, who was bringing destruction. Jerusalem would burn, even if Zedekiah could manage to pull off the greatest upset in military history.

Why did Zedekiah want Jeremiah to pray? _____
_____
_____

Jeremiah Is Arrested and Imprisoned

The lifted siege allowed Jeremiah to conduct some personal business. He tried to leave Jerusalem for Anathoth, his hometown, to take possession of some property (37:11-12) – undoubtedly the property he purchased before (32:9-12). But Irijah, a captain of the guard, stopped him at the gate on suspicion of treason. Supposedly, Jeremiah was trying to defect to the Chaldeans" (37:13) – an odd thing to do, considering the Chaldean army was no longer at Jerusalem. But given that Jeremiah was extremely unpopular in certain circles of power at the time, it is entirely possible that Irijah simply made up an excuse to get Jeremiah out of the way. Jeremiah was then beaten and jailed "in the house of Jonathan the scribe, which they had made into the prison" (37:15-16). It seems Jonathan's house had easy access to the large system of caves common to the Jerusalem area, and that a "vaulted cell" on his property was being used as a dungeon.

Zedekiah heard about the arrest, naturally, and he sent to have Jeremiah removed from the dungeon. That would seem to be a gesture of respect or even an apology. But as always, Zedekiah was more interested in his own problems than Jeremiah's. "Is there a word from the LORD"? he asked again (37:17). And he asked "secretly" – that word comes up more than once with regard to Zedekiah's support of Jeremiah. Of course, the word was the same as it had been – Babylon would conquer, and Zedekiah would suffer (37:18).

Having answered the king's question, Jeremiah takes the opportunity to plead his case. He had committed no crime (37:18). He was not deserving of the treatment he had received. He even suggested Zedekiah find the prophets who had been lying to him all this time and get their advice (37:19), since he obviously preferred their counsel. Zedekiah, moved by either compassion or terror, transferred Jeremiah to the court of the guardhouse instead of returning him to the dungeon; also, he told his jailers to make sure Jeremiah was fed throughout the siege (37:21).

Are our accusers always reasonable? If not, does it help to point out to them how unreasonable they are? _____
_____
_____

Sentenced to Death

Jeremiah may have reached his personal low (no pun intended) when his opponents finally convinced Zedekiah to authorize, or at least to avoid stopping, a sentence of death. Finally fed up with what they perceived as Jeremiah's persistent negativity, traitorous leanings, and hurtful speech, they petitioned Zedekiah to place him in their hands. Zedekiah, himself reaching a new low on a moral scale, said, "Behold, he is in your hands; for the king can do nothing against you" (38:5). That was preposterous, of course; the king could have done any number of things, just as he had done in times past. In short, he could have acted like a king. He chose not to.

The officials then threw Jeremiah into the cistern of Malchijah (38:6), evidently awaiting formal trial and condemnation. The cistern was dry in that it was useless for supplying water; however, the bottom was thick with mud. Judging from the fact 30 men were authorized to pull Jeremiah out, and twice the text indicates "worn-out clothes and rags" needed to be placed under Jeremiah's armpits (38:10-12), it appears Jeremiah may have sunk deeply enough into the mud to even endanger his life.

Thankfully, an Ethiopian eunuch named Ebed-melech intervened (38:7-13). He went directly to the king and told him what the king, surely, already knew – that Jeremiah was sure to die in the cistern before he ever came to trial. And the king authorized Ebed-melech to arrange for Jeremiah's release – release from the imprisonment Zedekiah could have prevented initially if he had spoken up earlier.

Why did Zedekiah's attitude vacillate so wildly? _____
_____
_____

Yet Another Audience with the King

After he ordered Jeremiah's release from the cistern and remanded him to the court of the guardhouse, Zedekiah set for Jeremiah yet again (38:13-14). He said, "I am going to ask you something; do not hide anything from me" (38:14). An odd request indeed. When had Jeremiah ever been accused of hiding information from the king? And when, upon sharing information with the king, had Jeremiah ever received anything but vilification and punishment? And as Jeremiah pointed out, Zedekiah had no history of listening to what Jeremiah told him anyway (38:15). But Zedekiah promised to protect Jeremiah, even swearing an oath in the name of God (38:16). But he swore "in secret" – a word that had already been used in reference to his respectful treatment of Jeremiah (37:17).

Knowing what Zedekiah would ask, Jeremiah answered him preemptively – if he surrendered to the king of Babylon, he and the city would be spared; if he resisted, the city would be burned and he would not escape (38:18). But although this was not new information, Zedekiah responded with a new reason for rejecting Jeremiah's council: "I dread the Jews who have gone over to the Chaldeans, for they may give me over into their hand and they will abuse me" (38:19). Could Zedekiah have been legitimately worried about the treatment his countrymen would give him in Babylonia? Or was he just making up yet another excuse? In any case, Jeremiah reminded him that the real concern was Babylon, not the exiles (38:20-23).

Zedekiah sent Jeremiah back to the guardhouse after warning him not to speak about the main content of their conversation. He said Jeremiah was only to say, if asked, that they had discussed Jeremiah's request not to be returned to Jonathan's house (38:24-26). Clearly Zedekiah was not swayed by Jeremiah's case, and he did not want to be accused of weakening in his stance. Jeremiah complied, and told the officials just what Zedekiah had asked him to say (38:27-28).

Did Jeremiah agree to lie? Is it acceptable to tell "part of the truth" under certain circumstances? _____
_____
_____
_____

Jerusalem Falls

In the 11th year of Zedekiah, after almost 18 months of siege and after the city had entirely exhausted its food supply, the Chaldeans breached the walls of Jerusalem (52:4-7). Just as Ezekiel had prophesied (Ezekiel 12:9-13), Zedekiah and the leaders of the people attempted to escape by night through holes in the wall, but Nebuchadnezzar caught them in the plains of Jericho, exacted his revenge on Zedekiah, and deported him in chains to Babylon (52:7-11).

The walls were broken down, and the city was ransacked and burned. Historically, soldiers who have attempted for extended periods of time to enter a city have been ruthless, bloodthirsty and rapacious upon finally gaining entry; there is no reason to suspect the Chaldeans were any more merciful than the norm.

Nebuzaradan, the captain of the guard, took captive most of the people. He left a handful of the rabble behind "to be vinedressers and plowmen" (52:16). Anything of value was taken, including the bronze implements, decorations and pillars from the temple itself (52:17-23). Note is made of three deportations conducted under Nebuzaradan. The first (52:28) is almost certainly that of Daniel. After omitting the largest contingent, which included Eze-kiel and Jeconiah (perhaps Nebuzaradan had no role), the text records two more relatively minor events (52:29-30). The timing suggests the first occurred when the siege was lifted temporarily, the second when the stragglers returned from Egypt after the fall of Jerusalem. We also have record of Jehoiachin, or Jeconiah, being shown favor during the reign of Evil-merodach (52:31-34). More than halfway through the 70 years of captivity, the Babylonian ruler granted mercy to Judah's last legitimate king and treated him as a royal in exile rather than a prisoner until his death.

Was Zedekiah's evil as bad as that of Jehoiakim and other evil kings of Judah's past (52:1-2)? _____

_____

_____

_____

Jeremiah's Story:
Finding Mercy

Exactly how and when Nebuchadnezzar became acquainted with Jeremiah is unclear. Per-haps it was when Jeremiah's letter went out to the exiles (29:1-3). What he knew, though, is more important than exactly when he knew it. By the time the walls were breached, Nebuchadnezzar knew enough to recognize Jeremiah as an ally, not a detractor. So he gave specific orders to his captain, Nebuzaradan, to not harm Jeremiah – in fact, to allow him to determine his own fate (39:11-12). So it came to be that a pagan ruler, not the king of God's people, released the prophet of God from prison permanently and permitted him free passage home (39:13-14).

Having the choice to stay in the wreckage of Jerusalem among the small remnant of survi-vors or leave for Babylon under Nebuchadnezzar's protection, Jeremiah chose the former (39:14). We are not told why. Considering the work Jeremiah continued to do for God in the aftermath of the invasion, including the entire book of Lamentations, it is reasonable to think it may have been at God's request.

Why would Nebuchadnezzar provide for Jeremiah? _____

_____

_____

Jeremiah takes this opportunity, by inspiration, to backtrack a bit and reveal how Ebed-melech also was promised safety when the city would finally fall. The Ethiopian eunuch had been instrumental in delivering Jeremiah from certain death in the muddy cistern (38:7-13), and God made sure his faith would be rewarded, "because you have trusted in Me" (39:18). There is no record of what happened to Ebed-melech, but can safely infer that God's assurances to him were kept.

Did Ebed-melech know God would save him when he rescued Jeremiah? _____
_____
_____

It is a sad comment that a lowly eunuch was able to do what the king of the nation could not: muster the courage to defend God's prophet against unfair treatment. On the other hand, Ebed-melech serves as a great example to us when we feel ill-equipped for a particular task of faith. It well could be that if we can do a little thing, and be seen doing it, God can provide the part of the deliverance that is beyond our capability.

How can we "lift up" faithful servants of God? _____
_____
_____

Key Image: Having His Life as Booty (38:2; 39:18)

Traditionally, nations have gone to war against other nations for the purpose of taking things of inherent wealth. Such prizes of war are often called loot, or booty. However, most men and women who have actually gone to war will testify that the real prize is returning home. Being able to walk away in good health is valued beyond all else. In the conflict between Judah and Babylon, Judah had no hope of any actual gain. But Jeremiah assured them they would be able to survive the conflict if they submitted to Nebuchadnezzar peacefully – and in so doing, win the biggest battle of all. Whatever Nebuchadnezzar might gain at Judah's expense would never be more valuable than that.

Key Image: Throne (52:32)

When Evil-merodach began to rule Babylon, he quickly instituted a policy of kindness – at least with reference to Jehoiachin (Jeconiah), the exiled Jewish king. After 37 years in prison, more than half of the promised 70 years of Babylonian captivity, Evil-merodach "set [Jehoiachin's] throne above the thrones of the kings who were with him in Babylon." This does not mean Jehoiachin was permitted to reign in any typical sense. But he was publicly recognized as royalty in exile rather than a mere political prisoner. He was given respect and good food. His "throne," therefore, refers to his status as king rather than any real power.

"Herod the king" (Matthew 2:1) and his descendant, Agrippa (Acts 25:24) were given kingly status under the auspices of Rome. This gave them considerably more leeway in dealing with their subjects than would have been the case under other local governors. It is possible that the liberated Jehoiachin was able to serve in some capacity as a political mouthpiece or arbitrator for God's people in his final days.

Key Verse: Jeremiah 39:18

"For I will certainly rescue you, and you will not fall by the sword; but you will have your own life as booty, because you trusted in Me," declares the LORD.

Key Lessons

- *Good news does not imply God's approval.* Blessings should never be used to justify rejecting God's will for our lives.
- *Power is useless unless used in the right cause.* The enthusiasm of sinful neighbors cannot be an excuse to forsake righteousness.
- *No pit is so deep that God cannot save us.* God can act on our behalf even when we cannot.

Lesson 10
Egypt
Jeremiah 40 - 45

Everything about Egypt was hateful to Israel. It conjured images of suffering, slavery and indignity. At no point was Egypt ever on the side of Israel. The marriage of Solomon to the daughter of Pharaoh (1 Kings 3:1) may have started him down the path of hedonism and idolatry that permanently broke the nation in half. Other nations that the Old Testament wants to depict as evil and oppressive toward the people of God are sometimes called "Egypt."

Strange, then, that the people were so desperate to return there.

Life After Desolation

Nebuchadnezzar had granted Jeremiah free rein to stay in Jerusalem or go to Babylon as he pleased, and he had chosen to stay (39:11-14). Nebuzaradan's offer is given in more detail in Jeremiah 40:1-6. This foreigner, sadly, showed more appreciation for Jeremiah's message than Jeremiah's neighbors. When Jeremiah expressed a preference for staying in Jerusalem, Nebuzaradan sent him to Gedaliah, who had been appointed by Nebuchadnezzar to administer the area on the emperor's behalf.

Jeremiah was not the only one seeking out Gedaliah. When word got around that the king had been deported and the government restructured, exiled Jews from all over came to Jerusalem to meet with him. Gedaliah assured them all that submitting to Babylon was in their best interest (40:9). In the meantime, he said, they should make the best of their situation. The ground was still fertile, and evidently not all of the vineyards and fruit-bearing plants had been destroyed; he sent them away to farm the land, and they "gathered in wine and summer fruit in great abundance" (40:12).

How could prosperity still be found in Judah? _____

_____

_____

The Scheming of Ishmael

Two of the men who came to meet with Gedaliah were Johanan, son of Kareah, and Ishmael, son of Nethaniah (40:8). At some point, Johanan had heard about a plot among the Ammonites to kill Gedaliah and stir up even more opposition to the Babylonians. Specifically, Johanan told Gedaliah that Ishmael was in the pay of Baalis, king of Ammon. Whatever evidence he may have had of this plot was not enough to convince Gedaliah, though. Johanan was prepared to assassinate Ishmael preemptively, but Gedaliah stopped him, calling the rumor a lie (40:13-16).

It appears Johanan's information was better than Gedaliah's instincts. Gedaliah welcomed Ishmael and his party with open arms and an open kitchen, and Ishmael repaid his hospitality by killing him, his entire entourage, and all the Chaldean representatives with him (41:1-3). The killing of a houseguest was perhaps the most egregious act possible in this culture. Lot was prepared to sacrifice his daughters' virginity to protect houseguests (Genesis 19:4-9). The betrayal of "my close friend in whom I trusted, who ate my bread" noted in Psalm 41:9 is generally thought to be a foreshadowing of Judas' betrayal at the Last Supper.

Ishmael is one example of a long line of extremists among the people of God, going back as far as Phineas (Numbers 25:6-8) and Jephthah (Judges 11-12) and continuing through to the First Century and men such as Theudas and Judas of Galilee (Acts 5:36-37). Historians call such ones, especially those who appear from this point in history forward, as the *sicarii*, or "knife-men." Today we would call them terrorists. Some of them, including Phineas and Jephthah, were working in accordance with the will of God, albeit in sometimes unconventional ways. Others were simply rabble-rousers and brigands with agendas that may or may not have been noble. The New Testament refers often to them as "zealots" – not in the sense that they simply were zealous for the people of God, but that they were motivated by their political agenda to bring down any Roman intrusion upon Jewish sovereignty. Simon the Canaanaean, or the Zealot (Matthew 10:4) was one of Jesus' apostles. Barabbas, who was released by Pilate instead of Jesus, was such a man (Luke 23:17-19), and the "robbers" on the crosses next to Him (Matthew 27:38) likely were as well.

What motivated Ishmael to turn on his fellow Jews? _____
_____
_____

Further Civil Unrest

If we were inclined, we could mitigate Ishmael's actions in the house of Gedaliah as those of an extreme nationalist, determined to right the wrongs inflicted on his people by ungodly foreigners and bring down the traitors who had empowered them. But it is difficult to see any positive side at all to the part of the story that comes next.

Before word had gotten out about Ishmael's treachery, a company of 80 pilgrims from various parts of the country arrived in Jerusalem to bring offerings in the temple – or at least, what was left of it (41:4-5). Their state indicates they had been through some of the worst parts of the Babylonian invasion and somehow lived to tell the tale. Ishmael made a point of greeting them and bringing them to meet with Gedaliah, only to slaughter them and throw their bodies down a cistern. The only ones to survive were those who claimed to have stores of provisions hidden, which Ishmael no doubt planned to take for himself (41:6-8).

This treachery of brother against brother is, no doubt, the reason Jeremiah specifically notes that the cistern chosen was one dug because of the warfare between Asa, king of Judah, and Baasha, king of Israel, many years before (41:9). We read in 1 Kings 15:16-22 and 2 Chronicles 16:1-6 how Asa, who generally is considered a good king, made an alliance with a foreign power so as to facilitate a war he planned on carrying out against his fellow Israelites. Clearly, fighting within the family of God long predated Jeremiah's day.

Ishmael then took captive anyone who remained in Mizpeh and fled to the Ammonites (41:10). Johanan, no doubt wishing Gedaliah had listened to him in the first place, took what remained of the fighting men and chased Ishmael, catching him by the great pool at Gibeon. The captives were able to get away from Ishmael and join Johanan, but Ishmael escaped with just eight men (41:11-15).

What can prevent warfare between brethren? _____

_____

Another Petition, Different Petitioner

Johanan, realizing Nebuchadnezzar would retaliate against Judah for Ishmael's treachery, gathered the people in Geruth Chimham and began making preparations to flee to Egypt (41:16-18). But before final preparations were made, Johanan and the rest of the people made a point of seeking out Jeremiah and asking his counsel (42:1-3). As a public figure, Jeremiah would have been known throughout the community as one who had been proven right time and time again, one who could be trusted to reveal the word of God in its completeness. Jeremiah was glad to comply. Johanan and the others made a point of emphasizing their commitment to following his words, whatever they might be, swearing by the name of God that they would do as Jeremiah said, "pleasant or unpleasant" (42:4-6).

As was ever the case, God through Jeremiah told the people to stay put, trust in God's power and the mercy of the Babylonians, and to not flee to Egypt (42:7-22). He was quite specific; the horrors they thought they would avoid by going to Egypt would in fact find them there. The only way to be safe was to have faith that God would save them – that His power and providence would be greater than Nebuchadnezzar's wrath. Since ignoring identical advice had gone so poorly for Zedekiah, and since they were on the record as being prepared to do whatever Jeremiah advised, it would seem the decision of whether to leave for Egypt or not would be made automatically.

What a difference 10 days can make. By the time God had spoken to Jeremiah, the attitude of Johanan was completely different. Perhaps he simply had a change of heart. Perhaps he had assumed Jeremiah would approve the trip to Egypt and was never really committed to obedience at all. In any case, Johanan and all the rest angrily rejected Jeremiah's counsel, going so far as to call him a liar (43:1-2). In a story that was becoming all too familiar, people who claimed to respect God's word simply did what they wanted to do instead – in this case, entering the land of Egypt, going as far as Tahpanhes (43:4-7).

Why would they think Jeremiah was lying? _____

_____

Jerusalem Falls

Considering the fact that Judah went to Egypt in the first place because they didn't want to follow God's directions, it should not be surprising that they increased their fondness for idol worship once they arrived. Since they had not listened to Jeremiah and had burned sacrifices to idols, God had retaliated by burning Jerusalem (44:1-6). God, through Jeremiah, was trying to bring the people back – spiritually, and eventually back to prosperity as well. Unfortunately, the people seemed determined to keep Him from doing so. They had found new gods in Egypt and were busy worshiping them (44:7-10). Men and women alike were united in their rejection of Jeremiah's message and their honor for "the queen of heaven." In fact, they said, all the prosperity they had enjoyed previously was when they had made these sacrifices, and their woes began when they stopped (44:15-19). Of course, none of them were old enough to intelligently comment on how things had been in previous generations. They had simply chosen to revise history to fit their notions of how things should have been.

Jeremiah told them the exact opposite was true – that God had protected them when they had served Him, and He had allowed misfortune, including the current misfortune, to come upon them when they rejected Him for other gods (44:20-23). But since they were not inclined to listen to God, he told those who had pledged their allegiance to the queen of heaven, "Go ahead and confirm your vows, and certainly perform your vows!" (44:25). If they would not be loyal to the true God, let them be loyal to their idols. But he warned them, just as he had before (42:17), those who had thought to escape hardship by fleeing to Egypt would be ruined. If they would not swear allegiance to the one true God, only a small handful of them would ever again have the opportunity to do so (44:26-29).

Jeremiah promised a sign to them as well. Pharaoh Hophra would be delivered to his enemies in the same way Zedekiah was given into the hand of Nebuchadnezzar (44:30). Although no call to repentance is mentioned, we infer from the existence of the sign that God was hopeful the people would see the fulfillment of Jeremiah's prophecy and come back to God before it was too late.

Baruch, Jeremiah's scribe, had remained faithful all this time. He is used here as an example of what the rest of them could have been. Back when he had written down Jeremiah's prophecies in a book for King Jehoiakim (36:4), he had complained to the Lord about the treatment he had received (45:3). But the discomfort he was feeling was nothing compared to the destruction God would wreak in the nation as a whole. Perhaps Baruch had thought being brought to the attention of the king would create "great things" for him personally (45:5). But God warned him about desiring exaltation in a world that was about to be brought to disaster. The reward he would be given, and in the end the only reward he would want, was his own life (45:5).

Is it wrong to seek "great things for yourself" (45:5)? _____
_____
_____

Jeremiah's Story:
Finding Mercy

Jeremiah's days of public preaching did not end when he went with the exiles to Egypt. After arriving in Tahpanhes, God told him to take some large stones and hide them in mortar at the entrance of Pharaoh's palace there in the city. And when he did it, he was to make sure some of his fellow Jews were watching.

Why was it important that some of the Jews watch? _____
_____
_____

Jeremiah was giving a sign to His people. God had said, "Behold, I am going to send and get Nebuchadnezzar the king of Babylon, My servant" (43:10). Nebuchadnezzar had been doing God's bidding while afflicting the people in Jerusalem before, and he would be called upon to perform similar service in Egypt. Fears of Nebuchadnezzar had been misplaced; the people should have feared God instead. Because they did not, they felt compelled to flee to Egypt. Since they still were rejecting Him, Nebuchadnezzar would be summoned again. To emphasize this point, Jeremiah marked the exact spot on which Nebuchadnezzar would erect his canopy when (not if) he came to Tahpanhes.

What symbolism is seen in God choosing a place for Nebuchadnezzar to set up his canopy? _____
_____
_____

It is significant that, in the description of Nebuchadnezzar's invasion of Egypt, he specifically mentions how he would destroy "the temples of the gods of Egypt" (43:12-13). The gods that God's own people had felt were preferable to Him would not be able to protect their own temples; instead of sacrifices being burned on their altars, the altars themselves would be consumed in fire.

What does the image of the shepherd's garment mean? _____
_____
_____

Key Image: Egypt (38:2; 39:18)

It is impossible to overstate the importance of Egypt as a symbol for ancient Israelites. Egypt meant slavery. Egypt meant a return to the time they were not a nation. Egypt represented everything from which God had promised to deliver His children. Throughout the Old Testament, and especially in Deuteronomy as Moses cautioned the people just before entering the land of Canaan, their history in Egypt and their lives as slaves were put before them (Deuteronomy 6:21, et al). Symbolically also, Egypt is used to represent everything Israel had left. Hosea, particularly, used the word "Egypt" to refer to the oppressors of God's people in general, even those who did not come from the southwest (Hosea 8:13; 9:3, 6, etc.).

By choosing Egypt, the people were essentially choosing to reject God's calling. They were going back to the time when they were not a nation at all, before they knew the God of Abraham, Isaac and Jacob. Such had been the case for years, of course, but the literal trip back to Egypt makes their decision that much more apparent.

In Deuteronomy 17:16, God promised the people that they would never again go back to Egypt. But God's promises are always contingent upon the people's willingness to submit to their part of the bargain. God cannot be held to His promise to bless His people if they are determined to reject His blessings. And in any event, the "nation" that traveled to Egypt in Jeremiah's day was not the nation of Judah. They were barely larger in number than the family of Jacob that went to Egypt initially. Jeroboam did not negate God's promise when he fled for safety to Egypt (1 Kings 11:40), and the remnant of Judah did not negate it here.

Key Image: "My Face" (44:11)

The actual "face" of God cannot be seen (Exodus 33:20). God does not live in our universe; He does not exist within the realm of the five senses. When the text refers to God turning His face toward something, it refers to a person or event that has attracted His attention. Generally, this attention is negative rather than positive. The figure of speech is used earlier in Jeremiah 21:10. Other examples include Leviticus 17:10, Leviticus 20:5-6, Leviticus 26:17, and Amos 9:4.

Seeing God "face to face" indicates a fuller, deeper understanding of Him. In 1 Corinthians 13:12, a "face to face" knowledge of His will is promised to a future generation of Christians. The partial, piecemeal revelation given through the apostles, and other inspired speakers and writers would one day yield to a complete revelation of His will. We are blessed to be the recipients of that revelation every time we read the completed New Testament.

A full revelation of His nature will have to wait until we ourselves escape this realm and enter heavenly dwellings with Him. Fuller fellowship than we enjoy here is alluded to in the text; the throne scene in Revelation 22:4 describes the people of God dwelling in such proximity to Him that they can see His face. More literal language is used in 1 John 3:2, where we are assured that we will see our Savior in heaven "just as He is" because we will have been transformed to be like Him.

Key Verse: Jeremiah 42:6

Whether it is pleasant or unpleasant, we will listen to the voice of the LORD our God to whom we are sending you, so that it may go well with us when we listen to the voice of the LORD our God.

Key Lessons

- *Some people never learn.* Those who are determined to rebel against God will find opportunities to do so.
- *Safety is where God places it.* Our efforts to save ourselves must not conflict with His plan for our lives.
- *Don't make it all about you.* Life is not about whether you are suffering or exalted; it is about finding ways to glorify God, wherever you are.

Lesson 11
Justice
Jeremiah 46 - 51

The Old Testament, including Jeremiah, was written for the children of Abraham – and for us as well, as we read it to find examples of God's dealings with His people (Romans 15:4; 1 Corinthians 10:6). Consequently, most of the warnings, condemnations and punishments recorded in Jeremiah have to do with Israel and Judah. But all people of all nations stand before God at some point. Reading the pronouncements of doom against the alien nations as we see in the late chapters of Jeremiah reminds us of that fact.

God will mete out justice against His people who rebel, certainly. But by no means does He imply that He will allow the rebellious, wicked nations of the world to go unchecked. He has a plan for them as well, whether He reveals it (as He did with these nations) or not.

Egypt

The condemnations of the foreign powers found in Jeremiah 46-51 can be put in three categories. Egypt, the traditional foe of Israel and the nation to which the remnants of Judah had fled in the days after the fall of Jerusalem, stands alone and is dealt with first.

Egypt's downfall had begun already. Pharaoh Necho's attempt to assist Assyria failed at the Battle of Carchemish in 605 B.C. Since that time, Babylon had grown even stronger and Egypt weaker. But like Judah, Egypt would rebel against Nebuchadnezzar. Ultimately, as Jeremiah had prophesied (43:8-13), Nebuchadnezzar would reach Egypt, erect his tent there, and put an end to Egypt's insurrection.

The flooding of the Nile, which ended with the construction of the Aswan Dam at the end of the 19th Century, brought nourishment to the land of Egypt, helping it serve as the breadbasket of the known world for centuries. Jeremiah likened the surging Egyptian forces to the rising Nile (46:7-8). But in truth it is God who was rising, and His effect on the land would be catastrophic. Despite all the allies and impressed armies from the African continent that Egypt would bring to the battle, ultimately "that day belongs to the Lord GOD of hosts, a day of vengeance, so as to avenge Himself on His foes" (46:10).

Israel was assured of its own survival through all this turmoil (46:27-28). Although a "full end" would be brought to many of its contemporary nations, Israel itself would survive through its chastening.

What is a "full end" in this context? _____
_____
_____

Philistia and Moab

The next group of seven prophecies can be seen as a group – seven being the symbolic number of completeness. Many other nations existed at the time, some of which came in occasional contact with the people of God; it is reasonable to assume God had plans to elevate or diminish them as well. These seven prophecies effectively show God's involvement with the nations at large.

Philistia is known by Bible readers primarily from its occasional incursions into Israelite territory, particularly in the days of Saul and David. The Philistines primarily stayed near the coast of the Mediterranean Sea, building their nation through maritime trade. It is appropriate, then, that the armies from the north that would come to destroy them are described as waters (47:2). Their trading partners, Tyre and Sidon, were cut off by the Babylonians so as to keep Philistia from rendering aid. Eventually the great Philistine cities of Gaza and Ashkelon would fall as well (47:5-7).

Moab, one of the nations descended from Abraham's nephew Lot (Genesis 19:37), was a continual thorn in Israel's side. Even before the conquest of Canaan, Moab was trying to block Israel's success. The destruction of Moab was prophesied in Numbers 21:29; this may have prompted the Moabite king, Balak, to commission the prophet Balaam to curse Israel. Of course, God would not allow a curse to be pronounced against His people, and Balaam wound up blessing Israel instead (23:7-10). Jeremiah uses almost identical language in his own prophecy of Moab's downfall (48:46).

Why does Jeremiah reference the Numbers prophecy? Do both prophecies speak of the same destruction? _____

_____

_____

Ammon and Edom

Ammon, Moab's sister nation, had been even more trouble for Israel over the centuries. In Jeremiah's day, "Malcam" (or Milcom), the national deity of Moab, is said to have "taken possession of Gad" (49:1) in the absence of its rightful citizens. But Ammon, too, would be taken captive soon. The fertile valleys of which Ammon was so rightly proud would be harvested by the Babylonians. The reading in the New American Standard Bible, "Your valley is flowing away" (49:4) gives the idea of the river that created the lush pastureland rising up and taking the soil out of the valley entirely. Versions such as the New King James simply refer to "your flowing valley, O backsliding daughter." In any case, Ammon would not be able to provide for itself amid the terror God would bring from all directions (49:5).

Edom, the descendants of Esau, was the nation closest to Israel; yet rarely did the two nations coexist well. The single-chapter book of Obadiah speaks of the downfall of Edom as well. Scholars are split as to whether Obadiah writes of the same destruction as Jeremiah; in any case, both seem quite definitive about the complete stripping of the nation (49:9-10; Obadiah 5-6). The rocky crags that had protected small numbers of natives from vastly superior forces for centuries would not protect them forever (49:16). A "lion" would soon come into their pastures and chase Edom from them on God's behalf (49:19).

What is the meaning of the question, "Who is like Me?" _____
_____
_____

Damascus, Kedar and Edom

Damascus is probably the oldest continually inhabited city in the world. Perhaps it is not accidental that, although permanent and irrecoverable damage is promised to some cities and nations in this text, nothing of that nature is said of Damascus. It would, however, be burned to the ground, along with its fortified towers (49:27).

Kedar is almost certainly descended from Ishmael's second son (Genesis 25:13). Like most Ishmaelite tribes, Kedar inhabited the wilderness (Isaiah 42:11; Psalm 120:5). Hazor, which was perhaps a kindred tribe, once inhabited Canaan (Joshua 11:10-13) but had migrated eastward. These nomadic tribesmen would not be able to find a place too out-of-the-way for Nebuchadnezzar.

Elam, another Semitic nation (Genesis 10:22) that once inhabited Canaan (Genesis 14:1), would be scattered by the Babylonians (49:34-39). Eventually they would be incorporated into the Medo-Persian alliance that brought down Babylon.

How might these Gentiles be restored "in the last days?" _____
_____
_____

Finally, Babylon

After Egypt and the other seven nations receive their pronouncements, Jeremiah finally states what his readers had wanted most to hear: What of Babylon? Would the oppressing nation itself, which was benefitting from the wrath God was pouring out on other nations, be brought down itself? The answer, of course, was yes; part of God's plan to restore His people after 70 years of domination was the overthrow of Nebuchadnezzar's empire (50:4-7).

Ironically, the fall of Babylon was so complete and so quick, corroborating evidence from archaeology eluded scientists for centuries. God planned to make Babylon "completely desolate" (50:11-15). The nation that seemed so invincible would no longer be so. Nations were encouraged to "Draw up your battle lines against Babylon" because of its sin (50:14). As impossible as it had been for Judah to withstand the wrath of God shown through Nebuchadnezzar, it would be equally impossible for Babylon to withstand Him when its time arrived.

Why is virtually the same language used with regard to the fall of Babylon (50:44) and Edom (49:19)? _____
_____
_____
_____

Jeremiah's Story:
The Calamity of Babylon

Jeremiah takes us back in time again after rehearsing the way Babylon would be overthrown, back to a message he sent by way of Seraiah in the fourth year of Zedekiah when the king made a trip to Babylon. Jeremiah gave Seraiah a scroll upon which he had written "all the calamity which would come upon Babylon, that is, all these words which have been written concerning Babylon" (51:60) – presumably what constitutes Jeremiah 50:1-51:58 in our Bibles.

Why did such a scroll need to be written? _____

_____

_____

The exiles already in Babylonia were no doubt eager for news from home. But surely the thing they wanted to know most was whether they would be returning home and what God had in mind for their oppressors. By way of a previous letter, Jeremiah had already told them about the 70 years of captivity (29:10). Now he would be able to complete the message. He told Seraiah to read the scroll aloud to the people as soon as he arrived, confirming that it was the word of God that assured them of Babylon's eventual defeat.

What impact would this have had on the Jews in exile? _____

_____

_____

The last time Jeremiah had been told to write a message on a scroll, that scroll was deliberately destroyed by its intended audience (36:2, 23). Clearly that reaction was displeasing to God; we know that if for no other reason than Jeremiah was told to replace the scroll (36:28). Strangely, though, this scroll was to be destroyed deliberately by Jeremiah's chosen messenger. He told Seraiah to throw the scroll, along with a stone to weigh it down, into the middle of the Euphrates. This would symbolize the sinking of the Babylonian empire and the word of God that caused it to happen.

Why not save the scroll instead? _____

_____

_____

Key Image: Like Wine on its Dregs (46:11-13)

Because of Moab's location, it was left largely undisturbed by passing armies on the way to this place or that place. A side trip to crush an unimportant noncombatant nation made little sense. Jeremiah likened Moab to wine that had been left undisturbed, allowing the naturally occurring sediment to settle to the bottom of the bottle or jar. Even today, with improved methods of winemaking, wine is typically allowed to sit on its dregs and then later decanted.

The time would come shortly when Moab's storehouses would be emptied. The undisturbed wine, as it were, would be "disturbed" mightily, to the point of shattering the jars themselves.

Key Image: An Object of Horror and Hissing
(50:3, 13; 51:37, 41, 43)

Lacking better documentation, it is difficult to understand the idioms of the cultures of the past. Did people literally "hiss" at those with whom they wanted to show contempt? Or gnash their teeth (Psalm 35:16)? Or are these examples of figurative language? In any case, it is clear that the exposure and subsequent ridicule of certain ones in these societies were characterized by public and blatant demonstrations.

It had been Babylon doing most of the hissing up to that point. It was the destroyer of nations, making others "a horror and a hissing, and an everlasting desolation" (25:9). But God was already preparing to reverse Babylon's fortunes. The same insults cast upon others because of Babylon's might would be put upon Babylon itself (51:37-43). It would be so completely overthrown that a proper cornerstone would not be found (51:26) – perhaps simply referring to the extent of the devastation, perhaps referring to the futility that would meet any who would try to resurrect the kingdom of Nebuchadnezzar.

Key Verse: Jeremiah 50:32

"Behold I am against you, O arrogant one," declares the Lord GOD of hosts, "for your day has come, the time when I will punish you."

Key Lessons

- *God allows wicked people and nations to prosper temporarily.* We should not mistake prosperity for God's approval.
- *The degree of His punishment may not seem appropriate to us.* We need to trust in God's judgment, not our own.
- *Every negative moment is a learning experience.* There is no time we cannot find a way to draw closer to God.

Lesson 12
Lamentations

For good people, being proved right in a prediction of doom and destruction is not a good thing. Jeremiah's attitude was as far from "I told you so" as could be imagined. He was not in the mood to gloat; he was far more concerned over the downfall of his nation and the subsequent status of the city of Jerusalem. "Lamentations" literally means expressions of grief. The short book of Lamentations, a postscript of sorts to Jeremiah's prophecy, describes Jeremiah's grief process after the fall of his nation, and the hope that still rose in his heart that better days lay ahead for his nation.

Life after Desolation

Today's generation may have seen photographs of war-ravaged cities such as Dresden or Sarajevo, or even Hiroshima. Jeremiah must have viewed Jerusalem in the same way. He saw empty streets where once he saw constant activity. He saw destruction where once he saw beauty. Instead of the holy city of God, he saw only the results of God's righteous wrath. The enemies who once feared Jerusalem now mocked and ridiculed.

Human needs are reduced to the most basic levels in times of crisis. Bickering over social position and other, lesser "needs" tend to disappear when there is no food to be found; indeed, the valued things associated with wealth and privilege are gladly traded for a full stomach (Lamentations 1:11). That was the state of affairs for Jeremiah and the bedraggled remnant that came back from Egypt.

Jeremiah writes two speeches in the first chapter of Lamentations in which he speaks on behalf of the suffering nation. The first one, beginning in the middle of verse 11 and going through verse 16, emphasizes the role of God with regard to the nation's current circumstances. God, not Nebuchadnezzar, punished the nation. This is precisely the conclusion most of Judah had vigorously tried to avoid during Jeremiah's time as prophet; perhaps by this point people had finally begun to listen and believe. The second speech begins in verse 18 and continues through verse 22. Here the emphasis is on God's righteousness in judging Judah. Not only did God bring the calamity, but He was correct in so doing. By no means does our acknowledgement make Him any more accurate; however, realizing our own blame is a necessary foundation for building true repentance. The next few decades would be a severe strain on the nation, but reaching the proverbial bottom of the barrel would give the people a good opportunity to bounce back.

How would we feel if our nation fell as Judah did? _____

_____

_____

Starting from Scratch

"Enemy" is a hard word. The idea of God becoming an enemy of His own people (Lamentations 2:5) is difficult to accept. But there is no other reasonable way to explain His behavior.

He truly was making war against Judah every bit as much as He had against Egypt, Assyria, and any number of other nations that rejected His will. It might seem out of proportion for Him to go so far as to destroy His places of worship and altar (Lamentations 2:6-7); how can proper worship possibly take place without such things? But God clearly was telling His people that corrupted worship is just as bad as no worship at all. Was it productive for Him to cause visions to cease among His prophets (Lamentations 2:9)? Perhaps not, but giving the visions to Jeremiah and other righteous prophets had accomplished nothing anyway.

Jeremiah had warned them years before, "Do not trust in deceptive words, saying, 'This is the temple of the LORD, the temple of the LORD, the temple of the LORD" (7:4). Simply having a historical connection to God, or a family connection to God, or even participating in the things of God is no guarantee of righteousness – and by extension, no guarantee of God's approval. Surely the state of Jerusalem, as Lamentations was being written, is ample testimony to that fact.

How can this be a word of warning for the people of God today? _____
_____
_____

The Suffering of the Innocent

We understand the wrath of God when it is meted out directly against those responsible for the downfall of a society. But what about the children? What about the handful of righteous souls that might get caught up in the furor? Is it right that blameless ones be "punished," in effect, for the sins of others? This is one of the emotional arguments made by atheists to attack the concept of a God who is simultaneously all-powerful, all-just and all-loving. Surely such a God would not punish those who did not deserve it.

First, we should accept the obvious: Innocent ones do suffer, and they certainly did in Jeremiah's day (Lamentations 2:11-12). Jeremiah writes of prayers on their behalf going unanswered (Lamentations 2:18-19). Taking the text at face value – and, as gruesome as it may seem, there is no compelling reason to take it any other way – it even appears that, as was the case during the siege (19:9), young children were seen as potential food sources (Lamentations 2:20, 4:10). It is God, not Nebuchadnezzar, who is given credit for the death of the people, including the young (Lamentations 2:21).

Does this make God evil? No, it makes man evil. However it may have fit into God's plan, it was Nebuchadnezzar who waged war and spilled blood. God's ability to use evil men for His purposes does not excuse them from being evil. Since the fall, mankind has suffered for others' sins – Adam and Eve's sins initially, and countless others afterward. The way to fix the evil problem in the world is to fix mankind, not to fix God.

Is there a specific purpose behind "senseless" tragedies in life? _____
_____
_____

The Success of Sinners

Job's friend Zophar said, "the triumphing of the wicked is short" (Job 20:5). But it doesn't always seem that way. Worse, they see their victory as vindication for their anti-God lifestyle. The Jews' enemies now were able to mock them, with Jerusalem, "the perfection of beauty," smoldering in ruins (Lamentations 2:15-16). Paul said, "Do not be deceived, God is not mocked" (Galatians 6:7), but he meant mocked indefinitely and without consequence; in the short term, God is mocked mercilessly and relentlessly. And usually, the mockery is only an excuse to mock God's followers. Surely, according to human wisdom, God would not act in the way He appears to have acted. Therefore, there is no God – or at least, God can be dismissed – and His followers can be marginalized as being duped and deluded.

God's plan often makes little sense in the short term, even to the faithful. That is where faith becomes even more important. Instead of allowing our question to fester into doubts, we can trust all the more. "The Lord knows those who are His" (2 Timothy 2:19). No matter what may be happening around us or to us, He will provide for us in the way He sees fit – both in this life and the life to come.

How is God glorified when bad people prosper at the expense of good people? ___

_____

_____

_____

The Flawed Case Against God

The bottom line is, trying to make God the villain in this story is an exercise in futility. However righteous we may think ourselves to be, however morally superior we may think ourselves over our neighbors, no one can claim righteousness before God based on his behavior alone. "Why should any living mortal, or any man, offer complaint in view of his sins?" Jeremiah asks in Lamentations 3:39. Our task is not to determine whether our sins somehow merit the treatment we have received, but rather to "return to the LORD" (Lamentations 3:40). The prophet spends much of the last half of Lamentations 3 telling of God's righteous chastening. Remember, Jeremiah was a godly man by almost any standard; yet he makes no effort to distance himself from the sinful majority. Truly, "all have sinned and fall short of the glory of God" (Romans 3:23).

Our job as sinners is to repent, even when repentance does not seem to reverse sin's consequences (Lamentations 3:40-41). After all, we are not repenting so as to improve our lot in life, but rather to correct our spiritual standing before God. Prayer can be a challenge; it may seem that our prayers cannot penetrate the wall of God's wrath (Lamentations 3:44). But despite appearances, God is always available to those who are truly penitent (Lamentations 3:55-57).

Mercy is in God's nature. It may not seem that we are receiving much, or that we will ever receive any more. But in truth, God has come to our defense more times than we could possibly count, and we can have full confidence He will do so again – in His time and in His way (Lamentations 3:58-66).

Is complaint in prayer always a bad thing? _____

_____

_____

Jeremiah's Story:
His Personal Journey

People of faith, such as Jeremiah, find ways to persevere under trial. But that does not mean they do not have dark days. They do. And although we typically see Jeremiah as a force for righteousness in Judah's national struggle against idolatry and ingratitude, we also see Jeremiah's own personal struggles. We have no reason to believe the prophet was tempted to engage in the depravity he saw and deplored among his neighbors; however, he had times when the burden he was asked to bear seemed too much. Lamentations 3:1-18 shows Jeremiah focusing on his own trials rather than those of the nation. He winds up concluding that peace and happiness are gone forever, that his strength and hope had perished. We would assume these thoughts passed quickly, but certainly they were there for a time.

Do we ever resent God for not exempting us from hardship? _____

_____

_____

Jeremiah wrote Lamentations looking back at his despair, though, not from the midst of it. He remembered those thoughts, and he remembered what dispelled them: a reflection on the unending mercies of God. "His compassions never fail," he writes in Lamentations 3:22-23. "They are new every morning." No day ever dawns in which God does not love and provide for His people. It may take some extra effort to focus on His mercies at certain times, but that does not mean the mercies are not there.

In what situations is God "faithful?" _____

_____

_____

Jeremiah finally came to the point in his faith journey when he realized his hardships were not a curse or a sign of neglect – but more than that; they were a blessing. Suffering can be good, especially in one's youth (Lamentations 3:27-28). Instead of nurturing an attitude of resentment toward God, we should instinctively reflect on His constant love and mercy. The reason we become impatient with God in our times of trouble is that we are so joyful when the troubles are absent. Truly, "The LORD gave and the LORD has taken away. Blessed be the name of the LORD" (Job 1:21). God truly is good; sometimes, though, we have to wait to see the blessing He is trying to work in us.

How is it good to "bear the yoke" in our youth? _____

_____

_____

Key Image: Portion (Lamentations 3:24)

The idea of apportionment goes back to the days of Joshua and the Canaan conquest. Seemingly at random (actually, though, through God's providence), territory was given to the tribes of Israel. Levi got no land portion, though; God and their service to God was to be the Levites' "portion" (Numbers 18:20). Whatever God decided to give or withhold, the knowledge of His Divine care and oversight should have been enough for them.

Jeremiah was forced to do with much less than had been the case in previous times. As long as he focused on what he did not have, he drifted further from his root of faith. When he says, "The LORD is my portion," he is acknowledging that the presence of God, not the presence of the blessings He brings, is the true source of joy and contentment. No encouragement can match what comes from the realization of the fellowship we enjoy with our Creator and Benefactor. He blesses us from day to day in the way He sees fit, and we need to praise Him for that. As Jesus teaches us in Matthew 6:33, putting His service at the forefront of our attention is our primary task; in doing that task, we can be assured that the rest is safe in His hands.

Key Image: Blacker than Soot (Lamentations 4:8)

Fire creates ash and smoke. Both turn skin dark. It is wholly possible that the filth of Jerusalem was literally in the air to the extent that the returning Jews found themselves turning darker by the day. However, the much more important meaning behind the term is a spiritual one. The state of the nation before God had been blackened deeply, a steep decline from the "purer than snow" consecrated ones of the past (Lamentations 4:7-8). Spiritual uncleanliness had become the norm, not the exception (Lamentations 4:13-15). It was almost as if their sins had literally darkened them (Job 30:30; Lamentations 4:1, 5:10). Only sin can render something this dark; only God can cleanse it again.

Key Verse: Lamentations 5:19

You, O LORD, rule forever; Your throne is from generation to generation.

Key Lessons

- *Sin should be mourned.* Instead of obsessing over unfortunate circumstances, we should grieve over the sin that brought the circumstances.
- *God is righteous when He punishes sin.* No amount of our own righteousness can atone, even for the godliest of us.
- *Hardship is an opportunity for faith.* If the wicked can turn away from God, we can turn toward Him.

www.ingramcontent.com/pod-product-compliance
Lightning Source LLC
Chambersburg PA
CBHW081552040426
42448CB00016B/3298

*9 7 8 1 9 4 1 4 2 2 2 3 6 *